Retirement Done Right

DON'T JUST INVE$T... PLAN!!!!

Jeannette Bajalia

Petros Estate & Retirement Planning LLC
Believe in Better®
JACKSONVILLE, FLORIDA

Jeannette Bajalia/Petros Estate & Retirement Planning LLC
4655 Salisbury Road, Suite 100
Jacksonville, FL 32256
www.petrosplanning.com

Book layout ©2013 BookDesignTemplates.com

Ordering Information:
Quantity sales. Special discounts are available on quantity purchases by corporations, associations and others. For details, contact the address above.

Retirement Done Right/ Jeannette Bajalia. — 1st ed.
ISBN-13: 978-1514863640

This book is dedicated to all the clients we serve, and those yet to be served, better known as the Petros extended family, who have given me the privilege of guiding them through their retirement journey and sharing their lives with our team. We have been blessed beyond measure and we are all humbled by the confidence and trust you have put in the Petros team; none of us take lightly the responsibility we have to partner with you to help you achieve your dreams. As you navigate the journey of your retirement lives, I pray:

"My God shall supply all your needs according to his riches in glory by Christ Jesus." *Philippians 4:19*

Contents

Preface

I was still in my corporate career when 9/11 happened. As was my routine, I had arrived at the office around 7:30 that morning and had a brief team meeting. I had just come out of the conference room and was passing by a co-worker's desk when she said, "We are under attack! A plane just hit the World Trade Center!"

My immediate thought was that she was probably overreacting. I had a mental picture of a small, single-engine airplane losing its way over Manhattan. Maybe it was a foggy morning up there. An inexperienced pilot probably. Didn't a military plane once crash into the Empire State Building? Hadn't I read that somewhere? Just a tragic accident, I thought. However, when I saw the serious expressions on the faces of those who had gathered around a TV in the conference room, I knew it was no accident. The news people were saying that a passenger jet had hit the building, and it was a crystal clear day in New York City. Dense, black smoke was now billowing from two sides of the north tower. Whatever hit the building had punched a hole through it about three-fourths of the way up. Then, as we were watching, a second plane hit the south tower. We exchanged looks that were a mixture of incredulity and worry. Some called family members to tell them and see if they were safe.

"Turn on the TV, Mom," I heard a co-worker tell her mother. "We're under attack." Shortly thereafter, as if we needed more proof that an organized assault on our country was underway, a third airliner slammed into the Pentagon. Details of the terrorist attack began to pour in. All we could do was watch and listen, and the world as we knew it would be changed forever by the events of that day.

Anything Can Happen, Anytime

If America is anything, it is resilient. We bounce back. It's in our national DNA. The events of September 11, 2001, would leave scars, but eventually things would return to a semblance of normal. The airports would open, and the airlines would fly their planes again. We would have tighter security from now on, and we would pay for it with a little slice of our freedom — random luggage searches and longer waits in the boarding lines. We would also come to recognize just how small the world in which we live really is. An event occurring half a world away could impact our daily lives here within seconds. Calm could turn to chaos within minutes.

Before the twin towers fell, they were located just a few blocks from Wall Street, home of the New York Stock Exchange, which is regarded by many as the economic hub of both America and the world. When 9/11 happened, Wall Street — the actual street — was covered with debris from the collapse of the twin towers. It was understandable that the NYSE would not open that day. It was a little surprising, however, that it would be closed until September 17, or for four trading sessions — the longest closure since March 1933, when the country was at the height of the Great Depression. Some in our profession wondered if the barons of the "Big Board" closed the NYSE for that long out of respect for the loss of life, or if it was to prevent the collapse of what they knew was an economic house of cards. When the market reopened on Monday, September 17, 2001, the Dow Jones Industrial Average stock market index (DJIA) plummeted 684 points — the sharpest one-day decline in history up to that point.

Hindsight is 20/20, of course. The terrorist attack may have precipitated the market crash of 2001, but the economy was ripe for a recession anyway. The sudden shock of a terrorist bombing just lit the fuse. The economy was in transition. The raging bull market of the 1990s was ending. For almost a decade prior to this, the market knew only one direction — up. Now investors would face the steep and costly down slope of the opposite side. The dot-com bubble burst and the tech stocks of the NASDAQ were the first victims, dragging the rest of the market down with them.

In 2003, the stock market began licking its wounds like an injured animal. It appeared to be slowly rebounding, taking on new life. Some thought it was a return to business as usual. But the more cautious among us knew better than to trust a market that could be so quickly shaken from its moorings. We were right. What many thought was a return to the glory days of the 1990s turned out to be merely a five-year calm before the storm.

Housing Boom, Housing Bust

Anyone involved in the housing industry between 2001 and 2006 was a happy camper. Money was flowing like a river after a snow melt. Everyone from the lumber salesperson to the landscaper was humming, "We're In the Money." Mortgage lenders were handing out loans to anyone who could fog a mirror and show a pulse. And why not? The value of property was going up so fast that by the time a buyer signed the paperwork the purchase was worth thousands of dollars more. Who wouldn't want to build, buy and loan on a sure bet like that?

Interest rates were so low as to be negligible and exotic loans were the rage. No money for a down payment? No problem! You can get a second mortgage to finance the down payment. Those were called "piggyback" loans for obvious reasons. There was also the "No Doc NINA" loan, or "no documentation" and "no income/no assets." A good credit score and your signature were all that was required to purchase a home. The bank's real collateral — and this is what got them and the entire economy into trouble — was the value of the property, which could always be repossessed if the borrower defaulted. Interest-only loans were popular. Why bother paying the principal when the average stay in a purchased home was less than five years? Adjustable rate mortgages (ARMs) enabled millions to buy homes because of the super low initial payments that would contractually increase later, floating on the prevailing rate at the time.

Close to Home

Flagler County, located only a few miles south of the part of Florida where I work and live, was the fastest-growing county in the country in 2004. New homes and high-rise condominiums were springing up like dandelions after a rain. According to county records, Flagler issued more than 4,000 building permits in 2004 and more than 3,300 the following year. According to the U.S. Census Bureau, from April 1, 2000, to July 1, 2005, the population of Flagler County increased by a staggering 26,578, or 53.3 percent. Flanked by the Atlantic Ocean and bisected by Interstate 95, Flagler offered one of the last strips of undeveloped beach property on the east coast of the Sunshine State.

Did the building boom happen because the population grew, or did the population grow because of the attractive real estate opportunities? Maybe it was a little of both. There was a lot of "flipping," or building homes on the speculation of an easy resale profit. During the boom years, it was not uncommon for a $400,000 home in Flagler County to appreciate more than $100,000 in the 12 to 18 months it took to go from the initial paperwork to the final inspection. A flood of investors leveraged cheap and easy credit to speculate on the basic economic law of supply and demand.

What was happening in Flagler County was typical of what other "hot spots" around the country were experiencing, especially in California, Florida and other sun-drenched states. But the law of supply and demand is a two-edged sword that cuts both ways. Free-enterprise-loving Americans seem to have a penchant for turning a good thing into a great thing and then into an unsustainable thing. Bubbles inevitably burst, and we are left picking up the financial rubble like so much confetti after a party.

Housing prices peaked in early 2006, started to decline in 2006 and 2007, and reached new lows in 2012. On December 30, 2008, the Case-Shiller home price index reported the largest price drop in its history. Borrowers with adjustable-rate mortgages couldn't refinance and began to default. Foreclosure signs were sprouting in front lawns across America. According to the general consensus, the credit crisis resulting from the bursting of the housing bubble led to the "Great Recession" of 2007 – 2010. Zillow.com©, a website that keeps track of home values, listed the 10 cities in America that suffered the steepest decline in property values when the housing boom turned into a bust:

1. Merced, California — 69.4 percent decline
2. Stockton, California — 63.8 percent decline
3. Modesto, California — 63.6 percent decline
4. Las Vegas, Nevada — 60.7 percent decline
5. Fort Meyers, Florida — 60.3 percent decline
6. Vallejo, California — 58.9 percent decline
7. Port St. Lucie, Florida — 57.9 percent decline
8. Bakersfield, California — 57.5 percent decline
9. Salinas, California — 57.2 percent decline
10. Melbourne, Florida — 56.7 percent decline

Too Big To Fail

The chickens circling the henhouse in 2007 came home to roost in 2008. Giant investment banks like Bear Stearns, Lehman Brothers, Morgan Stanley and Goldman Sachs would soon occupy the headlines of the nation's newspapers. These banks, which represented the heartbeat of the nation's economy and were considered "too big to fail," were doing just that. Their foundations had been eroded by what would soon become known as the "subprime mortgage crisis." Bear Stearns, the venerable "old reliable" of the banking industry, was the first domino to fall in March 2008 when it was swallowed up by J.P. Morgan Chase for pennies on the dollar. The deal was backstopped by the government which would later have to bail out J.P. Morgan Chase.

The metaphor "house of cards" was used more than once to describe the Wall Street mess in those days when we held our breath every morning waiting for another of the "too big to fail" banks to toss in the towel. The "bail or fail" list included Lehman Brothers, Merrill Lynch, Fannie Mae, Freddie Mac, Washington Mutual, Wachovia, Citigroup and American International Group (AIG).

On Monday, September 15, 2008, the Dow Jones Industrial Average dropped 504.48 points on the news that banks were running out of cash and couldn't pay off credit default swaps they had issued against mortgage-backed securities. The stock market was like an oil barge on the rocks, and nothing could stop the spreading sludge. Panic continued the following Wednesday. On September 17, money market funds lost $144 billion, and the Dow fell another 449 points. The largest one-day drop in history occurred on September 29, 2008, when the Dow fell 777.68 points. The Dow would eventually bottom at 6,594 from its pre-recession high of 14,164.

The Human Side

Toward the close of 2008, I saw a headline that read: "240,000 Jobs Vanish in November." I remember thinking that I knew some of those people who were out of work. Some were owners of businesses that served the building trades. One was a contractor facing bankruptcy. A few months ago he couldn't find enough workers, and was complaining about a shortage of materials. Now the new neighborhoods which were a beehive of activity were motionless; the staccato sound of pounding hammers gone. They were calling what we were in a "recession." What was it President Harry S. Truman said? "It's a recession when your neighbor loses his job. It's a depression when you lose your own."

According to figures from the Federal Reserve, total U.S. household wealth fell by about $16.4 trillion of net worth from its peak in spring 2007 — about six months before the start of the recession — to when things hit bottom in the first quarter of 2009. Again, those are just numbers until you translate that into people losing their homes and having to live with relatives until they can "get back on their feet." Just to make it through these rough times, some families combined to become multi-family households. We even saw the emergence of a new trend: the "sandwich generation," where as many as three generations began living under the same roof. Baby boomers who were "empty nesters" before the Great Recession now lived with returning children and aging parents.

As a financial counselor (or as I like to call it, a "financial coach"), I felt like a first responder to a disaster scene at times during the aftermath of the 2008 crash. My clients — thank God — were OK because we always protected their assets using customized, nontraditional strategies that withstood the economic storms, as well as the turbulence caused by unexpected life events.

I work with people who are either planning for retirement or who have already retired, and we make it a point to keep those precious, non-renewable assets out of harm's way. Others, however, were not as fortunate. Some who came to my office during that time were like victims of a financial tsunami. They were dazed and in shock with lots of questions.

"Why didn't my broker tell me this sort of thing could happen?"

"Why didn't anyone see this coming?"

"What do I do now that I don't have both my job **and** my nest egg?"

Some of these were individuals and couples who had lost as much as half their life's savings in the crash. Americans nearing retirement were hurt worst in that financial cataclysm. Aside from the $2 trillion gone from retirement accounts, the timing of things could not have been worse for them. These were people who had been saving and investing all their lives. Their brokers were telling them to "hang in there" because the market "always comes back." Or, "It's only a paper loss." I don't know about you, but anytime I ever see a negative return on my statements I never think it's only a "paper loss." These were people who didn't have time to recover from such losses, paper or otherwise. Their dreams were shattered. They were at the point in their lives when they would have to live on the wealth reflected in those paper statements. They weren't students of the stock market. They had trusted others to look after their financial affairs and, understandably, many of them felt betrayed.

I'll never forget one Monday morning when I got a frantic call from a 77-year-old woman with whom I had been working. I had encouraged her to reposition her assets into more conservative financial instruments. She was an intelligent woman, but her assets were invested as though she were a 40-year-old working professional instead of someone who was into the second decade of retirement. She fully intended to make those adjustments, but she had procrastinated and now was caught by the collapsing stock market. It was simply bad timing, but the financial setback she experienced caused her such emotional stress that she ended up in the hospital with a rapid heart rate and dangerously high blood pressure. Sounding hysterical on the phone, she said she needed help immediately. Sadly, while I told her that I could help moving forward, the damage done was irreversible. When we again met in person, we put some recovery strategies in place, but none of this would have been necessary had she not been following the advice of a financial advisor who had his head in the sand and was not sensitive to this woman's age and financial timeline.

Education Is Key

Could it happen again? I'm going to go out on a limb here and say that it is not a matter of whether but when. No one, no matter what they tell you or what they may imply, can see into the future these days. No one can predict the unpredictable and know the unknowable. It was a gift of God to prophets during Bible times that He has not seen fit to bestow on modern man. I don't mean to be cavalier, but the only crystal ball I have is a paperweight that says, "Excellence is an Attitude." I received it at a business convention... and that's all it says.

I would love to have been in a position to warn people who were in too much risk in the stock market to get out just before the last crash. But I didn't see it coming just as no one else saw it coming, regardless of what they are saying in hindsight. The difference between me and the financial advisors in whom those who lost half their fortune put their trust is that I would never have let them do that. And neither would those advisors, had they shown more concern about their clients' financial health and well-being than their own. What happens on Wall Street is as much a cycle as the ebb and flow of tides — just not as predictable. So what do you do if you know you are dealing with an erratic pattern? You adjust your expectations to it.

Plan — Don't Just Invest

The decision to write this book did not come in those dismal days of economic collapse or even in their recessionary aftermath. I decided to write this book when I noticed the mood of investors and those saving for retirement beginning to revert to the same rose-colored optimism as before the last collapse. One on one, and in whatever public forum I find myself when called upon to speak on the topic, I encourage those who are retiring to please please please plan for their financial future, not just invest. There is a big difference between the two, and the rest of this book will be about that.

I want to put in permanent form a few of the bedrock principles that will save those contemplating retirement from the financial ruin they could encounter by following bad advice. If you bought this book expecting to find a chapter entitled: "Ten Hot Stock Tips" or "How to Get Rich," I will help you get a refund. It's not that kind of book. I have nothing to sell here. I have no philosophical agenda to promote and no political axe to grind. If my faith in God and the Bible shows through a little bit here and there, I can't really apologize for that. It's who I am and one of the reasons I feel so strongly about reaching out and transforming the way pre-retirees and retirees are served by the financial services industry. It's my personal mission and passion, and I will not ever apologize for that.

This book is also not a sequel to my first book, *Wi$e Up, Women!* (published in 2012 by Advantage Media Group), although some of the more golden points made in that book may surface as nuggets in this one. What you will encounter in the pages that follow is intended to pull back the curtain, so to speak, on methods and strategies of retirement planning that many are not aware of for the simplest of reasons — they haven't heard about them. I wish I had a dollar for every time one of my planning sessions ends with, "Why didn't *my advisor* tell me that?" They are usually referring to a *better* path to retirement success, a *better* strategy to accomplish their goals, dreams and vision for the future, a *better* course to steer around the hazards that endanger so many in today's financial landscape. Thus, the comparative title *Retirement Done Right.*

Thank you for reading this far and as you continue, I would ask this: Keep an open mind. The strategies you will see expressed here are not merely based on my opinion, but are ideas and ideals that can be backed up by case studies, expert opinions of respected professionals, actual experiences and math. Some of the solutions presented here will not necessarily be those embraced by the mainstream. Thinking outside the box is often the only way to avoid dead ends.

Special ladies get special treatment on Valentine's Day...And every day!

CHAPTER 1

Finding a Need and Filling It

I had to chuckle the other day when I saw a bumper sticker at a traffic light. I could read the top line just fine: *"If what doesn't kill you makes you stronger..."* I had to squint to make out the bottom line in smaller type: *"...then I ought to be able to bench-press a Buick!"*

Challenges in life have always been a constant with me but, as the bumper implied, they have made me stronger, I believe.

My father, Elias Bajalia, was a good man and a hard worker. He had never been sick a day in his life until he suffered a massive heart attack and died at age 62. He had come to America from Palestine shortly after World War II. Like most immigrants, he wanted to make a better life for himself and his family in America, the land of opportunity. He was a shoemaker by trade, but here shoes were made in factories, so he opened up a grocery store and made a go of that. My first job at age seven was helping him run the store. I was his sidekick whenever I was not at school, stocking shelves, bagging groceries and ringing up sales at the register.

My parents were working class people who did not believe in life insurance. Dad died when I was 26 years old, leaving nothing behind for my mother but a $545 monthly Social Security check and me to take care of her and my great-aunt. When my great-aunt immigrated to the United States, she left with just the clothes on her back. She had nowhere to go but to our home. It was a family tradition with us to care for not only our immediate family but our extended family as well. When I graduated from high school at 16, I went straight to work as an executive secretary for a major insurance company — Prudential — the day after I graduated. College was out of the question. There was no money for such frivolous endeavors.

But I worked hard at my job and by the time I was 21 had moved into middle management. I suppose my crowning achievements there were moving around the company, holding 12 different assignments in 13 years of employment, and using creative problem-solving to fix whatever needed immediate attention in each of the departments. It was no easy task, but I discovered that I had a knack for creating solutions and implementing them. In my second career, I spent 24 years at Blue Cross and Blue Shield of Florida where I served in several leadership positions. My primary focus was creating consumer-driven health plans and helping the company develop business models around them. It involved putting all the right people together and slicing through walls of bureaucracy that sometimes seemed impenetrable. In the end, both the company and the members benefited — something of which I am still proud.

In the end, I did get a university education. I took advantage of a company-sponsored program that paid my tuition, and went to night school at the University of North Florida in Jacksonville, majoring in industrial psychology for my undergraduate studies and in human resources management for my master's degree. My family obligations were often confining, but I preferred to think of them as a responsibility instead of a burden. Caring for my great-aunt and my aging mother gave me what you might call a "higher order of purpose." It motivated me to work hard and save diligently, both for them and for my own eventual retirement. Who would have ever thought that an early family crisis and unexpected family responsibilities would lay the foundation for a professional journey that would make protecting families my life's work?

Becoming a Financial Advisor

When I began my career in the insurance world, I was just a kid, and I knew nothing about investing or managing money. When my company implemented a 401(k), I was excited.

"Let me get this straight," I said to the human resources representative. "Whenever I make a contribution, you match what I put in, 50 cents on the dollar?"

"That's essentially it," she said.

It didn't take a genius to figure out that the smart thing to do was save every penny I could. I couldn't believe my ears when I learned that some of my co-workers wouldn't even participate in the program! I was just miffed at the fact that the government put a cap on how much we could save. It was a no-brainer. The company contribution was free money. Every dollar I saved was a dollar that wasn't taxed. Those dollars grew untaxed in a market environment that was a win/win situation. If the stock market went down, my contributions bought more shares of the investments. When the market went back up, those shares increased in value. As long as I was pumping money into the program on a steady basis, I couldn't lose!

I contributed as much as I possibly could. When I got a raise, I contributed more. The self-imposed discipline of resisting excessive spending and saving every available dollar paid off. My great-aunt died in 1999 at the ripe old age of 101, and my mother passed away in 2006 at 93. By that time, I had spent 39 years in corporate America and had managed to save a tidy sum — more than $1 million. It is sometimes strange how fate's fickle finger points our lives in certain directions. Figuring out how best to invest that nest egg is what eventually led to my becoming a financial advisor.

After my mother passed away, I began thinking of making a change. I was 55, and I was contemplating the "what ifs" of "cashing in my chips" and leaving the corporate world behind. I decided to make that move in 2007. I was going to... for lack of a better word... *retire!* But somehow that word just didn't fit me at all. According to the dictionary, the word "retire" is synonymous with expressions such as "withdraw," "recede" and "fade away." That was not what I intended to do with the rest of my life. I did not exactly know which direction life after 50 would take me, but I sure wasn't about to pick out a comfortable rocking chair and take up knitting!

I had no intentions of becoming a financial advisor. I was not even sure what the term meant. I did need some financial advice, however. When I left my corporate job, I had a choice of allowing my defined benefit pension pay me a stipend for life or take a lump sum instead. I opted for the lump sum, figuring that I could invest it and come out better in the long run. I cashed out my 401(k) account as well, knowing that, because it was qualified money (the taxes had been deferred) I had 60 days to move it into another qualified account or face an enormous tax bill. But I had lots of questions. I did not know if I would need to continue working or not. How long would my million dollars last me? Life is full of unexpected twists and turns, and there were a lot of "what ifs" I needed some advice on. I needed someone to show me (a) where I stood financially and (b) what my financial future could look like. My list of questions looked something like this:

- How much savings would I need to have in order to comfortably retire?
- What could I expect in the way of a guaranteed lifetime income?

- How could I protect myself from unexpected expenses, such as health care?
- Should I pay off my mortgage?
- When should I take Social Security?
- What legal documents did I need to have in place?
- Was I sufficiently insured?
- Were my assets secure?

In short, I wanted a comprehensive *plan.*

I Googled "financial advisors" and started the process of interviewing five local professional financial advisors (at least that is how their websites advertised them) to find out how I should position my finances in the most prudent manner possible. To my way of thinking, these were all logical, legitimate questions to which any thinking person would want to know the answers. I was confident that I would find those answers from the professional "financial advisors" on my list. Two of the five advisors came highly recommended by company executives and had been "hand-picked" to provide financial advice to the executive ranks. Naturally, I thought, "they have got to be good at what they do if other company executives use them." I could not have been more mistaken!

Not one of these "advisors" could answer my questions and offer me a comprehensive retirement plan. I had never been so frustrated! Where was the disconnect here? Each one I talked to wanted me to just leave my money with them and they would invest it for me. They showed me colorful pie charts and pointed out how my assets would be "diversified" among small cap stocks, large cap stocks, growth stocks, mutual funds and international investments. I wanted a fully integrated retirement plan, but what I got were portfolio presentations. Their focus was on investing, and I was asking for a plan! They were not listening to me; they just wanted to sell me their investments. There can be no doubt that investing is an integral part of financial planning, but where was the depth? Where was the roadmap to my financial future? I felt as if I was a traveler asking for directions to the interstate and no one knew what an interstate highway was!

"So let me get this straight," I said to one "financial advisor." You put all my money in the stock market, and you get to charge me a 2–3 percent asset management fee?"

"Yes, that's right. Per year," said the advisor.

"Whether my account goes up or down in value?"

"Yes, that's right."

Well, it wasn't right for me! I wanted more — I wanted a fully integrated plan that protected me for the rest of my life.

Doing what I do best — meeting with clients to design plans that can help them make their retirement dreams come true.

Joining Petros

Two expressions fit here: *"I was born at night, but it wasn't last night,"* and *"If it is to be, it is up to me."* For the next few weeks I asked friends and associates if they knew of any financial advisors who could do **comprehensive** financial planning. The trail eventually led to Petros Estate and Retirement Planning in St. Augustine, Florida. These were the first people who seemed to speak my language financially. The million dollars I had managed to save was not easy money. It had come through hardships and careful management, not a Las Vegas-style rolling of the investment dice. Phrases such as "asset preservation" and "conservative money management" were music to my ears. So were expressions like "guarantees" and "income protection." Hearing talk of guaranteed growth, instead of the pie-in-the-sky projections offered by the previous five advisors, was like a breath of fresh air.

In the process of my interview with them, Petros learned about my corporate background in the insurance industry. When they asked me to join their company, I was surprised and delighted. I agreed to do so as an independent contractor. I wanted to learn everything I could about integrated retirement planning and began by using my own situation as a test case. I set to work analyzing alternatives to lessen the overall risk to my estate while optimizing its growth potential at the same time. I also explored ways to legally and ethically reduce my tax liability. I set about developing a comprehensive estate plan and put in place strategies that would allow me to transfer my assets to my heirs in the most tax-efficient manner possible. I took it upon myself to identify resources at a national level for mentoring and coaching. I wanted to identify best practices and state-of-the-art, non-traditional protective strategies that I could integrate into retirement planning. During my time as an independent contractor, I realized that the owner of the firm was a sales guy — he only wanted to sell financial solutions. He had a one-size-fits-all model hidden behind his so-called "asset protection" approach. He went to the other end of the continuum, which was quite concerning. So I invented a fully integrated planning process based on customizing strategies that supported client goals. Imagine that! A financial model that was directly linked to a *client's* retirement goals, income needs and legacy plans!

In the 1980s, a Remington electric shaver commercial made Victor Kiam famous for the one-liner, "I liked it so much I bought the company." That was me. I liked Petros so much I bought the company! I had only intended to stick my big toe into the water of financial and retirement planning — just enough to find my own solutions. However, I soon became so intrigued with the process that it seemed a natural fit for me to take the training necessary to become a full-fledged retirement and financial advisor. It did not take me long to recognize that I wasn't the only one seeking answers to questions pertaining to retirement. Most people who had come to that juncture in their lives faced situations similar to mine. I soon learned that there was no end to the amount of good I could do, the number of people I could help and the lives I could financially enhance in this new career upon which I had stumbled. As the sports figures do when they leave the field of play, only to learn that they were happiest when they were in the game, I "unretired."

Dodging the 2008 Bullet

When I was interviewing the five "financial advisors," and they were recommending that I place my nest egg in the stock market (yes, ALL in the stock market), they had no way of knowing what was ahead. In just a few short months, economic disaster would strike. Wall Street would crumble under the pressure of the collapsing housing bubble. Some of their clients would lose as much as 50 percent of their life's savings in the 2008 financial crisis. Had I taken their advice, my portfolio, or what would have been left of it, would have been a victim of that meltdown. Looking back, I don't think those financial advisors made their recommendations maliciously; they simply didn't know any better. They were good people in a badly broken financial advisory system. They were merely operating within the scope of their education and training. They were extremely limited in the strategies they could offer. Their responsibility was to their employer, who told them what investments to sell to their clients. Their idea of diversification was to sprinkle the assets into different types of risk. That didn't change the fact that it was still *all at risk!* They were merely behaving according to what the famous psychologist, Abraham Maslow, called the "law of the instrument" — "If the only tool you have is a hammer, you tend to see every problem as a nail."

Those people were like a broken compass. They could only point in one direction because that was the only direction they knew. I do not necessarily hold it against them; I'm just glad I had the instinctual presence of mind not to take their advice. Like fish in a small aquarium, they were very well acquainted with their environment but nothing else beyond. Under their system, I would have had no guarantees that my money would last throughout my lifetime. The experience impressed upon me how much the financial services profession was under-serving baby boomers who, with limited recovery time, could not endure a market hit in the later years of their retirement. It was also under-serving another segment of the baby boom generation — those who, like me, found themselves in the role as caregivers either for aging parents or children returning to the nest because of some dramatic life change, like loss of employment or a broken marriage. The aforementioned "sandwich generation."

"Find a Need and Fill It"

Most of my college courses were boring and tedious. One professor, however, was capable of saying things that made you want to write it down, underline it and draw circles around it. She was making the point that, in the free enterprise system, there is never a vacuum because the key word is "enterprise."

"Find a need and fill it," she admonished us, "and you will always have a job to do."

I discovered that at Petros, I didn't need to go searching for those needs. They were self-evident with most people who walked in the door. Seniors who were in or approaching retirement all had similar concerns:

- Have I saved enough to retire comfortably and safely?
- Where can I invest my savings with safety and good growth?
- What happens if there is a divorce or the premature death of a spouse?
- What about legal protections?
- Is there any way around the probate nightmare?
- How can I easily transfer an estate to my heirs?
- How do I keep up with skyrocketing health care costs?
- How can I protect my estate from being eaten up by the cost of long-term care?
- How can I keep the IRS from inheriting 50 percent of my estate?
- How does inflation get factored into my plans?

There was a lot of crossover between my corporate life and my second career at Petros. At Prudential, I was involved in estate protection and the financing of capital needs through life insurance and annuity families of products. When clients lost a spouse or experienced an unfortunate life event, they needed to find some way to pay for things like their mortgage or a child's college education. In many ways, it was the same, familiar turf of finding the right tool for the job, or, like doctors sometimes do, putting the patient (client) with the right specialist for the job.

My first widowed client, who was my inspiration to create Woman's Worth®, poses with me.

Clients dressed for the occasion at our Christmas Open House — food, fun and friends.

CHAPTER 2

What's All the Hype About Retirement?

To officially qualify for baby boomer status, you must have been born between 1946 and 1964. This is the generation that statisticians refer to as the "pig in the python" because of the way the graph looks when it shows the curve in the birth rate between those years. The line was somewhat flat through the Great Depression and World War II, but then, when the soldiers came home from making the world safe for democracy in 1945, they did what comes naturally and started families. The birthrate swelled upward, peaked in the late 1950s and tapered off to normal in the mid-1960s.

The impact baby boomers have had, and are still having, on the world's economy is profound. Expanding families needed new houses, cars, TVs and refrigerators. As a consequence, the postwar American economy grew like a tall tree — one which has been offering shade and produce to the rest of the world for decades.

Now, the generation that gave us rock and roll, the space race and flower power is retiring. Is it any wonder that so many commercials on TV are aimed at the gray-haired segment of the population? It's where the money is! It is also no wonder that the bookshelves and magazine counters are overflowing with advice on retirement. Have you noticed how many cable TV channels are devoted to financial analysis these days? We are experiencing a retirement advice avalanche that started in the late 1990s and shows no signs of abating. By some estimates, as many as 10,000 baby boomers are turning 65 every day. To put that in perspective, EverBank Field, the stadium where the Jacksonville Jaguars play professional football, has a total capacity of 73,000. If the stadium were full (we can always hope), and you could stand on the 50-yard line of EverBank Field and take in a 360-degree scan of the seats, roughly that many people are retiring every week in America. All of those people are making financial decisions right now that will affect the quality of their retirements for years to come.

I think it is fair to say that the need for education in this area is greater than ever.

Planning Ahead

I remember seeing a framed poster on an office wall once with the words PLAN AHEAD on it. What made the sign unforgettable, however, was that all the letters were the same size except for the last two, which were smaller and closer together. The ironic inference was that the sign painter had run out of room due to lack of planning.

Sadly, most Americans spend more time planning a two-week vacation than they do planning their financial futures. When researchers ask American baby boomers if they are ready for retirement, the answers are not encouraging. The Pew Research Center took a survey and discovered that 60 percent of baby boomers ages 50 to 61 say they may have to postpone retirement. They don't think they can afford to stop working.

An index released in February 2014 by Natixis Global Asset Management ranks America only 19th globally for retirement security. The USA is lagging behind much of Europe, including the Czech Republic. Switzerland leads the pack in this category according to NGAM, closely followed by Norway.

Statistics from the U.S. Census Bureau put the average savings of a 50-year-old in the U.S. at $43,797. Here's two more Census Bureau statistics I found troubling: The percentage of Americans over 65 who will rely solely on Social Security in retirement — 35 percent. The percentage of people ages 30-54 who believe they will not have enough money put aside for retirement — 80 percent.

Challenges Facing Retirees Today

I attended a seminar one time where the speaker said there are three kinds of people in this world:

Those who make things happen.

Those who watch things happen.

Those who say, "What happened?"

That clever little aside does make the point that you need to be proactive when it comes to your financial future. I have heard the challenges associated with retirement compared to many things: climbing a mountain, sailing the sea, dodging bullets, crossing a minefield. Some of those sound dire, don't they? My favorite metaphor, however, is taking a journey along a trail where you may encounter obstacles or challenges. You are more likely to succeed if you have the services of a guide — someone with local knowledge — to help you plan for and overcome these obstacles. Some of the possible challenges facing retirees today are:

Outliving your money

What would you say would be on the top of the list of what seniors fear most? Snakes? Spiders? Dying? Would you believe running out of money in their old age? According to a poll taken by the Allianz Life Insurance Company of North America, when they took a sampling of people ages 44 to 75, the fear of depleting assets outranked dying or anything else as their biggest fear. And yet this is really only a risk if you fail to plan. Any risk during retirement can be managed. Notice I said it can be managed, not necessarily avoided. Some risks cannot be avoided.

It's not uncommon for men to spend 30 years in retirement and women even longer. Baby boomers are living longer on average than any generation that preceded them. The fastest growing segment of the population in America is a 90-plus generation. You may attribute it to better medical care or better lifestyle habits, but there is a 25 percent chance that the husband or wife of a married couple age 65 will live to age 95. It's a good challenge, but a challenge nonetheless, because it calls for a deliberate plan to manage your nest egg carefully and strategically to make sure you don't run out of money in retirement.

Since you could have as many as 30 years ahead of you in retirement, doesn't it make sense to determine how much you need to sustain your lifestyle and enable you to achieve your dreams and retirement goals? Once you have that figure, you can work backward. But if you don't know the cost of your retirement, then you don't know how to position your money to work for you *in* retirement. You really don't want to wake up one day in your 70s or 80s and realize the money cupboard is bare, you have run out of resources and you are stuck living solely on your Social Security. And yet this is the impending fate of many folks when they go into retirement without a plan.

Skyrocketing inflation

Even with the burst of runaway inflation the nation experienced in the late 1970s and early 1980s, the average inflation rate since World War II has been a manageable 3.1 percent. But think of what would happen if you were, let's say, 10 years into your retirement, and your budget was finely tuned to your income, and along comes this inflation tsunami such as the one that occurred when Jimmy Carter was president in 1979. Could it happen? Anything could happen. Even a 3.1 percent inflation rate takes a bite out of your retirement resources. Imagine 3.1 percent compounded. That's great on the receiving end, but not so great when you are having 3.1 percent compounded *subtracted* from your overall wealth — which is what inflation does.

One of my clients asked me to visit with her brother who happened to be in town. It seems they were having a chat about retirement planning, and he had some questions that she wanted me to answer. We had a nice discussion. He said that he and his wife were both age 58, and he wanted to retire at age 65. He wanted to know how much he would need to have in his nest egg in order to accomplish that goal.

He was surprised to see the impact inflation would have on his financial picture. The numbers don't lie. He was spending roughly $12,000 per month. By the time he retired, with inflation figured in, that figure would jump to $14,800. With the amount he had saved to date, he would run out of money by age 79. Since this was just a neighborly chat and not an official planning session, we didn't go deeper into possible strategies that would enable him to lock in a guaranteed income for life, although with the amount he had accumulated he was well-positioned to do so. One thing stood out in his mind, however. He could negate the effects of inflation by a combination of paring down his expenditures and boosting his savings.

Retirement and financial planning isn't rocket science, but it is science, which comes from the Latin word meaning "knowledge" or "awareness." You have heard the maxim, "Forewarned is fore-armed?" In planning for retirement, it is oh, so true!

Unpredictable interest rates

As long as we are listing "X, the unknown" factors that could impede our retirement journey and cause us problems, we have to acknowledge interest rates. We financial people often speak of the "interest rate *environment*" as if it is a pervasive atmosphere that is always subject to change. ***That's because it is!*** As I write this, interest rates, both for borrowing money and interest rates paid on savings, are at an all-time low. The unpredictability of interest rates poses the greatest threat to retirement. But even this can be addressed with proper planning.

When you move into your retirement years, money has a different purpose. Money is no longer what you save to get you ***to*** retirement; its purpose now becomes what it can create for you in terms of lifestyle and ***security*** during retirement. So if you are going to depend on interest rates to supplement retirement income for the lifestyle you have spent more than 30 years dreaming about, you can be sadly disappointed when those interest rates suddenly change. Some of our parents and grandparents anticipated living off interest from bank certificates of deposit. Those days are gone. Twenty-first-century retirees need a plan that provides guaranteed income streams irrespective of the prevailing interest rate environment. This is where some insurance industry products excel. Income annuities have become very popular with baby boomers because they provide income guarantees that are not dependent on unpredictable interest rates. Chasing interest rates is no way to retire and poses great risk to a dignified, successful retirement.

Stock market fluctuations

I've never been to Adventure Landing in Jacksonville Beach, Florida, but I'm going to guess, just based on my knowledge of human nature, that if you go there and find your way over to the *Wacky Worm* roller coaster, you will not find many over the age of 50 standing in line, waiting to ride. Advertisements for the *Wacky Worm* and the other thrill rides at the park make the following promise:

> *"Thrill Rides flip you, spin you, twirl you, drop you and toss you. Some spin to the point where you can hardly stand. Others flip you upside down over and over and over again. And a few drop, leaving you with nothing but butterflies in your stomach."*

Young investors with time on their side can handle the roller coaster ride of the stock market just fine. The last thing older investors want to do, however, is have all of their resources at risk in the stock market and get caught in market meltdown followed by a prolonged recovery and a lingering bear market. The financial consequences could be disastrous, not to mention the emotional and psychological damage done by stress and anxiety at a time in your life when you should be living a worry-free life of abundance with your family and friends and pursuing recreational interests.

The economic cycle of bull markets and bear markets continues and will continue ever more irrationally as we become more interdependent on global economics. In fact, as this is written, we are due for another major market correction, based on the history of the market, which is something no one needs in their retirement years.

A comprehensive retirement plan can protect you in this regard. The plan would identify how much of your retirement nest egg you need to have positioned in the stock market and for what purpose. Every situation is different, but one strategy that seems to be a favorite of Petros clients is to segment money into three buckets that provide safety, liquidity and growth. The growth bucket is the only one that needs to be in the market. Every retiree needs money in the market, but only the right amount as dictated by your retirement plan, which is, or should be, driven by your goals and dreams. In my personal retirement plan, for example, I chose to have 25 percent of my assets in bucket one for emergencies when I encounter them. I have 40 percent in bucket two — my guaranteed income bucket. This bucket uses five laddered annuities to provide income at various stages to keep up with inflation, escalating health care costs and the possibility of long-term care. The remaining 35 percent is in the stock market. In my case, I want that much in the market for growth, and that's all I want to put at risk. Why? Because, quite frankly, that's all I need to have at risk and still protect and preserve my retirement lifestyle.

Finally, while we are on the topic, a word of caution about trying to play catch-up. It is tempting for some to take too much risk with retirement money when they feel like time is running out, and they have not met their savings goals. They take on too much investment risk in the hopes they can boost their portfolio. Trying to make up for lost time in such a manner can be a recipe for disaster. I do more than 50 planning reviews each month and what I see is that more than 80 percent of the clients I serve are taking too much risk when a "perfect storm" like the one we experienced in 2008 could be right around the corner.

I completed a review for a 72-year-old woman who did not have a plan and suddenly began to worry about running out of money. What sparked her concern was all the talk about Obamacare and how much her health care may cost her going forward. She had 83 percent of her assets in equities, and her advisor had placed those assets in only two asset classes, each with high fees. What was even more intriguing was that the remainder of her money was sitting in a money market account earning only .005 percent interest. She did not have a plan; she simply had investments. When you are ready to retire, your retirement plan should drive every financial decision.

If I could build what I'm about to say in cinderblock letters 40 feet high, paint them traffic cone orange and put purple neon lights around it for emphasis, I would: **AN INVESTMENT PORTFOLIO IS NOT A PLAN.** I can't be any plainer than that.

Rising taxes

Whenever I get onto the subject of taxes as a guest and local trusted advisor on my weekly radio show, *The Financial Safari*, I have to bite my tongue to keep from getting on a soap box about how what's happening at the regulatory level affects this area of our financial lives. So I won't get on my editorial soapbox here. But I will say this. You can count on taxes going up. If you need proof of this eventuality, see me in person, and I will show you just what I mean. But this is a biggie when it comes to planning. I know of no other area in the financial universe where the uneducated are penalized more. This is particularly true among retiring baby boomers, where the majority of their nest eggs are invested in tax-deferred accounts like 401(k)s, 403(b)s or IRAs. That's a sure plan for tax disaster. One of my mentors is Ed Slott, the nation's foremost authority on IRA distribution planning. I am one of his credentialed Master Elite Advisors. I agree with him wholeheartedly when he refers to these accounts as an "IOU to the IRS."

The IRS code contains four million words. If it were an actual book, it would be four times thicker than Leo Tolstoy's iconic wordy novel *War and Peace*. The U.S. tax code is twice the length of the Holy Bible and the entire works of Shakespeare combined. Yet, hidden in its multitudes of sections and paragraphs are gems that can literally save you thousands upon thousands of dollars if you know where to look for them.

Like most Americans, I am patriotic. I want to pay my fair share of taxes. But I think I am also like most Americans in that I don't want to pay a penny more, and I sure don't want to pay someone else's taxes for them. I love to see smiles spread across the faces of clients when they learn that, simply by applying a perfectly legal and entirely ethical provision made possible by the Internal Revenue Service, and published in the IRS code, they can shave thousands of dollars from their tax bill.

If you have most of your retirement nest egg in tax-deferred accounts like IRAs, 401(k)s or other employer sponsored plans — look out! You have created a time bomb that can explode during retirement. The only thing that can prevent such a derailment is proper planning.

As I write this, the president's 2016 Fiscal Year Budget Proposal has more than 10 proposals for changes to retirement account savings, Roth IRA distribution changes and other elements, the aim of which is to get at retirement savings. Whether this is enacted remains to be seen. I for one don't intend to sit around and wait to see what happens. I do not worry for my clients because we're on top of it and have taken taxes into consideration in their retirement plans and, in the planning process, we look at taxes from an entirely different perspective.

What some don't realize is that their advisors can create tax problems for them by not even bringing up the subject when they are putting investment strategies on the table. This is especially true with strategies involving taxable money. The client only begins to discover this, however, when they begin using these accounts for income in retirement. You need a plan for this.

I'm really not singing — I'm preaching! The sermon topic: "If you fail to plan, you plan to fail."

CHAPTER 3

What Does It Take to Do a *Complete* Retirement Plan?

When I turn on the TV, it is usually to either catch up on the day's headlines or do what I call a "brain drain," which means watching something inane to put my mind in neutral after a long day at the office. I typically zip through commercials, or tune them out entirely, but one about retirement caught my attention recently. The announcer says, "We asked people a question, 'how much money do you think you will need before you retire?'" The camera zooms in on a hand with a marker, writing "$500k" on what looks like the end of a wide strip of yellow ribbon. Another hand writes "$1 million."

The announcer says, "We gave each person a ribbon showing how many years that amount might last," as the camera zooms out to show a large group of people of all ages, each holding one end of a yellow streamer. One end of this yellow ribbon has been tied to a stake and the people are walking away from the stake in all different directions toward "age markers" — age 65, age 70, age 80... all the way to age 100. The length of their ribbon must have been determined by the figure they wrote down. As these people are walking away from the center and outward through the concentric circles that represented their ages attained in retirement, some of them run out of ribbon. That seems to have been the point of the commercial. Some of them ran out of ribbon and were surprised their money didn't take them any farther. The commercial was cleverly done. It showed one young man tugging on his ribbon, saying "Can I just pull it a little farther?" Obviously he had guessed low. A woman is shown pulling the end of her ribbon to the "age 70" marker and says to the camera with a serious look. "I'm going to have to re-think this thing."

The announcer comes back on and says, "It's hard to imagine how much we will need for a retirement that lasts 30 years or more. So maybe we need to approach things differently if we want to be ready for a longer retirement."

The camera then zooms out to show the participants stretching a blue ribbon beside their yellow ribbon. The blue ribbon seems to stretch all the way to age 100. Happy ending.

The commercial, which I think was put out by an insurance company, made a good point. A few generations ago, the idea of a retirement lasting 30 years or more would have been absurd. Not today. As mentioned in the previous chapter, people are living longer; the fastest growing segment of the population is the 90-plus generation. So the reality is this: retirement is no longer a single-dimension planning opportunity. It has many facets that must be considered to determine how much you will need for that dignified, dream-filled retirement for which you have spent more than three decades saving. Unfortunately, what is tripping up many baby boomers is that they have not been saving with a finite goal — one derived from intelligent and comprehensive planning — in view. This is even true for some parents of boomers, because they never dreamed they would live this long.

At the Rate You're Going, You'll Be 100

Former *Today* show weatherman Willard Scott was best known for showing pictures of people over the age of 100 on their birthday. People who live to be 100 or more are called *"centenarians."* As of the 2010 census, there were 53,364 centenarians living in America. What's interesting is that in the period from 1980 to 2010, the centenarian population experienced a larger percentage increase than did the total population! In 1980, the number of those over the age of 100 was only 31,194. Centenarians increased 51 percent from 1990 to 2000. Do we see a trend here? Some think that by the 22nd Century, so many will be living to age 100 and beyond that it will no longer be newsworthy.

According to *Prevention* magazine, the increase in longevity (up 30 years in the 20th Century) is the greatest gain in 5,000 years of human history. Whether it is attributable to progress in medical science, safer foods, or better lifestyle habits, what is amazing to scientists is the gradual upward climb.

The way mortality tables work, the longer you **have** lived, the longer you **will** live… on average. For example, according to the Social Security Administration's actuarial life table, a male aged 55 can expect to live another 25.29 years, or a little past the age of 80. If he makes it to age 70, however, he can expect to live to age 84. Women living to age 70 will, on average, live to age 86.[1]

According to the study, "Older Americans 2012: Key Indicators of Well-Being," in 2010, there were 40 million people age 65 and over in the United States, accounting for 13 percent of the total population. The older population in 2030 is projected to *be twice as*

---

[1] Social Security Administration. "Period Life Table, 2010." http://www.ssa.gov/oact/STATS/table4c6.html. Accessed June 2, 2015.

large as in 2000, growing from 35 million to 72 million and representing nearly 20 percent of the total U.S. population."[2]

Good news/bad news

If you had to list what you thought were the top five challenges to retirees in the 21st Century, would you include longevity? If you are considering the financial aspects of retirement, how could you **not?** It is the quintessential good news/bad news story. I have good news: You are living longer! I have bad news: You are living longer! Let's face it. It takes money to maintain the quality of life most of us envision when we enter retirement. The alternative is to become either a ward of the state or a burden on our families, neither of which is acceptable from the point of view of a professional planner.

Ignoring the elephant

The majority of financial planners are not addressing longevity. I know investment advisors are not including this very real challenge in their asset management practices. It reminds me of those three monkeys you see sometimes illustrating the old adage, "Hear no evil, see no evil, speak no evil." One of the monkeys covers his eyes with his hands, one covers his mouth and the other puts a finger in each ear. That's one way to avoid the obvious "elephant in the room" — just pretend it's not there and maybe it will go away. Longevity begs the need for deliberate strategies that are customized to ensure you **will not** run out of money before you run out of time.

I strongly advocate taking at least a portion of your wealth and converting it to an infinite income stream, one that will still be

[2] Federal Interagency Forum on Aging Related Statistics. 2012. "Older Americans 2012: Key Indicators of Well-Being." http://www.agingstats.gov/. Accessed June 2, 2015.

generating a paycheck for you even if you live to be 120. Every case is different based on your life goals, your lifestyle needs and your legacy planning needs, but it may not be as difficult as you think. Several strategies exist in the world of financial planning for just that purpose, and one of them will probably fit your situation. But, buyer beware! If a strategy is being implemented for you without it being directly linked to a detailed and customized retirement plan, *run the other way!* You don't need to be sold financial solutions that are not linked to your personal goals. Your individual, unique personal goals are what should drive *every* financial decision you make.

Most so-called financial plans I see are nothing but a group of investments put together and called a plan. These investment plans come with the typical asset allocations in place to accommodate growth and inflation, but they miss the mark on investment solutions that address the issue of longevity. The risks associated with longevity are far greater than any market risk, particularly with the passage of the Affordable Care Act, which became law in March 2010, with full implementation scheduled for 2015. Talk about your fiscal cliffs! As this is written, we are just now seeing the financial impacts of this legislation — with more to come!

To give longevity the real treatment it needs in a financial plan, it takes a village and every skill and capability that the village contains. At Petros, we use a team of experts to shape our longevity planning process. We call it Retirement Lifestyle Protection Planning®. It reminds me of a complex surgery where several doctors are involved, each one responsible for a different area of concern. The primary surgeon may have responsibility for the success of the operation, but he or she will be depending on the help of the anesthesiologist to keep the patient stabilized during the operation. A cardiologist may eye the beeps and blips of the heartbeat and blood pressure monitors if the surgery involves the cardiovascular system. An internist may be especially attentive to what medication is required for the patient to fully recover. Then there is an entire team of surgical assistants who are there to respond to any and all the needs of the primary surgeon as directed by him or her. We believe that your retirement lifestyle deserves the same care and commitment to success.

In a retirement income and financial planning session, it should be a common practice to call in specialists where the situation demands. Planning for longevity is a process that requires integrating tax planning, income planning, health care planning and estate planning. We have found it necessary to move away from the traditional three-bucket process and add a fourth bucket where we cover the contingency of increasing health care costs that could potentially deplete a client's portfolio.

To quote the late Beatle, John Lennon, "Life is what happens to you while you're busy making other plans." Successfully planning for the future requires that we first visualize the future as best we can, knowing that things may change as we move through time. We all have 20-20 vision when looking at the past; we don't see what lies ahead with the same crystal clarity. But just because we can't chart all the contingencies perfectly doesn't mean we shouldn't have a plan at all. We do the best we can with the knowledge and the tools available to us to chart our financial future. It's called being prepared.

For example, we know by looking at the past that inflation will likely average between 2.5 percent and 3 percent per year. Actually, the 100-year average of inflation is 3.2 percent, just in case you want to be precise. It would be foolish not to take that number into consideration when planning for our incomes 20 years out. To reason that because we don't know the exact number we cannot plan is foolish and irresponsible if you care about your loved ones. What our Petros team does is huddle on each case and agree on the likely scenario associated with it based on the information gathered on each client. Every case is unique, don't forget. Taxes can be projected and trimmed using estate-planning strategies. Rising health care costs can be anticipated and measures taken to offset them. Other possible unforeseen events that could have a financial impact, such as the loss of a spouse or a debilitating illness, should at least be addressed with comprehensive Retirement Lifestyle Protection Planning®.

The estate planning piece requires "crossing the t's and dotting the i's" on an overall retirement and financial plan. No one lives forever. To quote William Shakespeare, we will all one day "shuffle off this mortal coil." Or, as country singer Hank Williams put it, "I'll never get out of this world alive."

Once we understand this, the only responsible thing to do is make our plans accordingly so that our loved ones will be cared for when we walk out on life. And we are not merely talking about buying insurance here. There are countless strategies and combinations of strategies that can be employed to ease the financial burdens of those you leave behind. One of these strategies usually fits hand-in-glove with your unique financial situation.

On a daily basis, I see people walking around thinking they have a financial plan when all they have are investments and insurance products which have been sold to them by so-called financial advisors who had little knowledge of or interest in their goals, dreams and desires. That is a sure way to fumble your retirement. Your goals should come first — then products and strategies *if* they fit those goals.

I saw a bumper sticker the other day on the back of a motor home that boldly proclaimed, *"We are spending our children's inheritance."* It reminded me of a couple I once interviewed whose expressed goals were (a) to put in place a guaranteed lifetime income with a little cushion for contingencies, and (b) to spend every last nickel they had accumulated throughout their lives. They were serious! The man quipped that it would suit him just fine if the last check was to the undertaker and it bounced! Their two children were both well-educated professionals who were highly compensated. The couple had no other immediate family and they were not inclined to leave their personal fortune to any charity. They had a wish list of places they wanted to see, and things they wanted to do while they were active and healthy enough to do them. The planning process with this couple was different than most. Once we got their guaranteed lifetime income worked out, we then did a year-by-year plan on how they could spend their resources on their "wish list." I have never seen a couple so thrilled with a plan that was guaranteed to leave them broke. Well, not really... they would always have their guaranteed income, which was more than enough for the two of them for life.

Investing Is Running the Money

Once you have your plan, that's where investments come into play. You need proper asset allocation based on your age, your goals, your lifestyle, your income needs, your tax status and your legacy wishes. These investments need to be properly allocated and appropriately diversified. Some financial advisors are like the folks Abraham Maslow described. All they have is a hammer, so everything looks like a nail. When they say "diversified" they usually mean spread around in different sectors of the market, all of which come with a measure of risk. What I mean by "properly allocated" and "diversified" is to properly balance assets between equities and fixed income investments across every asset class available, not just an advisor's favorite one or two.

This is not a one-size-fits-all strategy; it is uniquely customized. In all the years I have been solving problems, I have yet to see one plan look exactly like another. Your goals are not the same as some TV celebrity, nor are they identical to your next door neighbor or your twin sister who lives in Seattle. They are yours and yours alone, and your retirement and financial plan should not be crafted so as to resemble anyone else's.

My passion is Retirement Lifestyle Protection Planning® with our client specialists and educating people about the difference between planning and investing.

CHAPTER 4

The Three Qualities of Money

As a little girl I learned many things from working with my immigrant father in our family-owned grocery store. It was one of the most valuable educations I ever received and I wouldn't trade it for any of the degrees and certifications I would later earn. My father believed in the goodness of people and never let the negative experiences he encountered destroy his faith in the overall uprightness of human nature.

One day while busy stocking shelves, I saw a small drama unfold. A woman came to the counter with her purchases and was digging through her purse for wrinkled dollar bills and coins to pay for them. It soon became obvious that she didn't have enough. While she was sorting through the basic food items she could do without, my father gave a dismissive wave of his hand, as if to say, "Don't be silly. You are a good customer. I know you will pay me when you can." Then he did something that I will never forget. He took a box and went to the shelves and put together what amounted to a "gift basket" for the poor woman. She thanked my father profusely, but again he gave her the "it's nothing" wave of his hand.

I learned from my father one of the most fundamental moral principles of life: It's better to give than to receive. I saw his passion to give back some of what he had received by coming to America. My father did not become rich in a material sense. He made a living, and that was it. But he was wealthy beyond measure in other ways and I was far richer for having had his influence in my life.

At age seven, I stocked the shelves, took inventory, greeted customers, bagged groceries and, even though I had to stand on a stool to reach the keys at first, rang up sales on the cash register.

When I was in my teens, I actually helped my father run the store. One afternoon a salesman came selling signs, most of which catered to the grocery business, like "Two for the Price of One" and "Fresh Picked"... that sort of thing.

There were other signs with pithy little sayings, like, "In God We Trust — All Others Pay Cash!" and "Helen Wait is our Credit Manager. Need Credit? Go to Helen Wait." My father took one look at those signs and walked away, leaving me to deal with the salesman. Although he hadn't said a word, I knew he considered the signs rude and offensive. One of the signs, however, made sense for a small store like ours. I didn't buy it, but I always remembered what it said.

"Great Service, Low Prices, High Quality — *Pick Any TWO.*"

Ours was a small business. We did not have the buying power of the supermarkets on the outskirts of town, so we couldn't compete with their prices. Then again, those guys couldn't compete with us when it came to the excellent quality of our meats, fruits and vegetables. These were personally selected each morning by my father from the farmer's market on Beaver Street. Nearly all the produce we sold in our small store was grown by immigrant farmers who had picked it the day before. The meats came from the local butchers. Of course, there was no way the mega-markets could duplicate the cheerful and friendly service our small family store could provide.

The Perfect Investment?

The "pick any two" idea also applies to investing — "Safety, Liquidity and Growth — *Pick Any Two.*"

Once, when I was speaking to a small audience at an estate planning workshop, I went to the whiteboard with marker in hand and asked them to give me their idea of a perfect investment. The list went something like this:

High Returns — Of course! If you are going to invest your money it only stands to reason that you want a return on your investment.

Safety of Principal — In other words, you like the idea of high returns but you don't want to lose what you invested. Makes sense.

Liquidity — You want to be able to get at your money when you need it.

It made perfect sense. The perfect investment would have liquidity, safety and growth. In the real world, however, it's like that sign — "Pick Any Two." When it comes to investments, a kind of trade-off exists.

Take the stock market for example. You have the opportunity for some great growth with the stock market. When economic conditions are right, and all the gears of industry and commerce are turning and spinning, it is not uncommon for the stock market to produce returns of 30 percent or more. A great investment for growth, right? But what's the downside? Almost overnight, those gears can grind to a halt and kick into reverse and you can lose 30 percent or more. Great growth potential but not safe. Liquidity? Imagine a hand waggle from me here. You have to sell shares of your holdings and convert them to cash, but the money usually shows up in your checking account by the end of the trading day and that's pretty good on the liquidity scale.

Banks are safe. Accounts are insured by the FDIC up to $250,000. Checking accounts these days cost you money unless you keep thousands of dollars in a minimum balance. Savings accounts offer such miniscule rates of return that most people say, "Why bother?" The rate of return on certificates of deposit has dropped to a fraction of a percent as this book is written. You are not even keeping up with inflation. Those who remember the glory days of CDs when you could get 3- and 4-percent returns call CDs "certificates of disappointment." So, no growth potential here. But what do you have? Great safety and liquidity. Like the sign said, "Pick Any Two."

Real estate is an investment. There is great growth potential in real estate if you know what you are doing. What is it they say? Location, location, location? As one client said to me with a chuckle after he had closed the deal on a beach cottage, "God ain't making no more land!" Is it safe? Give it another hand waggle here. Historically, it has been. Try telling that to those who became victims of the 2007 housing bubble collapse. But real estate is considered a stable investment. The element that is lacking in real estate investments, however, is liquidity. You have to list the property and find a buyer before you can turn it into cash — a process that can take months, even years in some cases. You don't want to end up with all your eggs in one basket, as the old saying goes. Many baby boomers did just that when they listened to their parents,' who advised them from their historical perspective — "invest in property; you can't go wrong." Some have found themselves property rich and cash poor in the modern economy of the 21st Century.

From a retirement income planning standpoint, you need all three of these "money qualities" represented in your portfolio, so the key is to have the right blend of all three of them.

Three Buckets

I want you to visualize three buckets of money. The first bucket has the word "LIQUIDITY" stenciled on it in big red letters. You will have easy access to this money for the next, say, three or four years. We will call it our "rainy day" bucket.

The next bucket has the word "SAFETY" painted on it. This bucket starts out with very little in it. When you are in the accumulation phase of your economic life, and time is on your side, you can afford to take more investment risks. But as you grow older, you begin to move more and more of your money into this bucket. The money you are saving for retirement is precious to you. It represents years of your blood, sweat and tears. More and more, the idea of losing it on some risky venture becomes unconscionable and unacceptable. Your SAFETY bucket fills more and more as you enter the distribution phase of your life where income planning involves replacing the work paycheck with the withdrawal paycheck. You add to SAFETY and remove risk as you progress through the various stages of your financial lives.

The "Rule of 100" helps us determine how much risk is acceptable in our portfolio. It is not a hard, fast rule, but rather a "rule of thumb," or an approximation. The way it works is this: Take your age and put a percent sign after it. That is how much money you should keep completely safe in your portfolio. The reason why it is call the Rule of 100 is because you can take your age, subtract is from 100, and that is the percentage of money you may have at risk and still sleep at night. In other words, when you are 60 years old, you should have 60 percent of your money in the safety bucket. This consists of those asset classes that give you guaranteed income streams that you will begin pulling from to maintain your lifestyle in retirement. At Petros, we use lifetime income annuities in this bucket because of their amazing ability to protect your assets and guarantee income. Simply stated, the SAFETY bucket becomes pension, an income you can't outlive — something every retiree needs in order to have peace and confidence, knowing their core lifestyle costs will be met regardless of any changes in the economic environment that may come along.

The third bucket has the word "GROWTH" painted on it and it is the money you need to have working for you in the stock market. Using our example of the 60-year-old and the Rule of 100, some 40 percent of his or her money will be in investments that bear a measure of risk, but they are well diversified and spread across 12 asset classes designed to mitigate market volatility. This is the bucket with money invested in the stock market. As you journey through a retirement which could very well last three or four decades, you are bound to encounter some periods of high inflation. This spawns rising costs. This portion of your portfolio is designed to keep pace with that. It is also there to offset other unknowns of retirement, such as increased taxes and health care costs. This is the bucket you won't need for the early stages of retirement, so you let it sit there and grow and compound.

Balancing Act

The key in all of this is to keep things in balance. When I was a kid, we watched the Ed Sullivan Show every Sunday night. Some of the acts were corny and downright silly. I never could figure out Topo Gigio. He (I suppose it was a he?) was this squeaky little puppet mouse who spoke with an accent. The little rodent must have had a contract with Mr. Sullivan that guaranteed frequent appearances.

Another regular was Erich Brenn, a master at spinning plates on sticks. He would get eight or 10 plates spinning, each of them perfectly balanced on the tip of a four-foot rod. Then, Brenn would juggle, or perform some other trick while one or two of the plates in the background began to lose their centrifugal energy and wobble dangerously close to crashing to the floor. Just when you thought a plate would fall, Brenn would save it in the nick of time. Meanwhile other plates began to wobble. The tension was part of the act of course. I would later read that Brenn spent hours between performances practicing the art of achieving perfect balance and timing with the spinning plates.

The same kind of meticulous balance and awareness of timing is required in successful investing. What I see is investors placing too much emphasis on dividend producing stocks as an income source. While this is a good tax planning strategy, without a plan to validate what else is needed, it can work against you if you have to liquidate stocks to handle a life crisis in your family. This is especially true if we happen to be in a bear market at the time. Or consider what can happen when corporations reduce dividends due to a bad economic cycle in their particular industry? You don't want to have your income dependent on such variables.

On the other hand, what doesn't get enough consideration is the effective use of income annuities in retirement portfolios. Not too long ago, I saw an article in the Wall Street Journal debunking the traditional 4 percent rule, or as it is sometimes called, the "4 Percent Withdrawal Rule."

"It's about time," I said to a co-worker. The "4 Percent Withdrawal Rule" died some time ago but many stockbrokers and other Wall Streeters are just now attending the funeral.

The Death of the 4 Percent Rule

The "4 Percent Rule" was born in 1994 when a California financial planner, William P. Bengen, developed an investing formula that would allow a retiree to withdraw 4 percent each year from a brokerage account for 30 years. Bengen's idea was to rebalance the account with a mixture of stocks and bonds and keep it growing while it continued to provide income. It was great in theory, but it couldn't stand the test of time. Stockbrokers loved it because it advanced the doctrine of trusting one's entire fortune to the stock market. To them, it was the Holy Grail of investing. The "4 Percent Rule" was developed in the 1990s, when the stock market was in an extended bull market. When the bears took over in 2000, the math no longer worked. Nobel-Prize-winning economist William Sharpe had this to say about it:

> *"Supporting a constant spending plan using a volatile investment policy is fundamentally flawed. A retiree using a 4 percent rule faces spending shortfalls when risky investments underperform, may accumulate wasted surpluses when they outperform and, in any case, could likely purchase exactly the same spending distributions more cheaply."* [3]

Many in the business of selling stocks, bonds and mutual funds couldn't accept the fact that the investing doctrine around which they had built their sales pitches was false at its core. As the decade that began in 2000 wore on, even the die-hard adherents to the 4 percent rule had to admit that the math no longer worked.

The WSJ article mentioned above had been written by staffer Kelly Greene, who has covered retirement for the newspaper since 2000. She is known for her unbiased and well-informed opinions. Her research concluded that the best performing portfolios over time consisted, not of a blend of stocks and bonds, but a 50/50 blend of stocks and fixed annuities.

In the article, Greene quotes Wade Pfau, a professor who researches retirement income at the American College of Financial Services in Bryn Mawr, Pennsylvania.

---

[3] Jason S. Scott, William F. Sharpe and John G. Watson. "The 4% Rule — At What Price?" Journal of Investment Management. Third Quarter 2009. April 2008.

"Annuities, with their promise of income for life, act like "super bonds with no maturity dates," says Pfau, who holds a Ph.D. in economics from Princeton University.

The Golden Compromise

Insurance companies are not stupid. They understand that liquidity is important to seniors who have worked long and hard to accumulate their nest egg, and don't like the thoughts of locking that money up where they can't get to it in return for the security and potential returns an annuity can provide. Most carriers now allow for free withdrawals of 10 percent per year from the annuity balance during the surrender period. Also, surrender periods in most annuities have been reduced to 10 years.

As with the debunking of the 4 percent withdrawal myth, the media is sometimes slower to catch on than those of us on the front lines. What I think is all too often left out of the equation is the effectiveness of income annuities in that SAFETY bucket that can protect the assets of retired folks while guaranteeing them an income they can't outlive regardless of market conditions.

More and more advisors are recommending annuities because of the demand placed upon them by modern retirees for guarantees, not projections. The "4 Percent Withdrawal Rule" was all projections. All we have to do is look back at the decade which began in 2000, and the two major crashes it spawned, to see that projections can fail.

The adage "once bitten — twice shy" comes to mind when I think of the attitude among older investors who witnessed the crash of 2000 and the financial crisis of 2008. Even though the stock market has made spectacular gains since then, the mood of most seniors seems to be like that of an earthquake survivor. They remain guarded, and rightly so. Not only *could* it happen again, market history dictates that it *will* happen again — we just don't know when. Investors who saw their retirement nest eggs implode view annuities and the income guarantees that come with them as quite desirable by contrast. Now that they are retiring, it's not so much the return *on* their investment that they worry about as it is the return *of* their investment. Since gambling on the stock market has fallen out of favor with boomers, and they are looking for guarantees, it is no wonder that the word "annuity" is surfacing more and more in conversations with once market-bound advisors. Ifs and maybes are great for talking purposes, but for the nuts and bolts of retirement planning you need guarantees.

The golden compromise allows for a little give in one of the three "money qualities" to accommodate the other two. Fixed index annuities, for example, allow you returns predicated on the upward movement of the stock market — thus added horsepower for growth. FIAs have a ratchet/reset feature that lock in those gains and prevent the account from losing ground during a market downturn — hence, safety. Liquidity concerns are assuaged by the 10 percent free withdrawal provision. It's the compromise between growth, safety and liquidity that makes it work.

Not all annuities are created equal, however, and you need to be aware that there are four generations of annuities — some really good and some really bad. Do not be sold an annuity contract if it is not directly linked to a retirement plan. I review annuity contracts daily for my clients who were "sold" an annuity but have no idea what is in the contract or how it will be used. If you were to give me 100 annuity contracts, I would most likely reject 97 of them as contracts that don't provide the highest value. Have you ever seen expert tasters sample wines or foods to determine the quality? I love being the "test judge" on annuity contracts. Some of them just don't pass inspection.

The Utopian Investment

I am not personally acquainted with anyone who has won a state lottery and become an instant multi-millionaire. When I read in the newspaper where a waitress or a taxi driver wins the lottery and vows to not let it change them, I can't help but chuckle to myself. It won't be long before the money will have its effect — and from what I read, usually an ill effect.

The people who promote the lotteries are thrilled when someone hits it big. It makes a big splash in all the newspapers and lottery ticket sales go through the roof with people trying to duplicate the miracle.

The same is true with the stock market. I'm sure there are a few who had the prescience to buy Apple shares when they were $22 per share in 1980 (Apple increased in value 10,000 percent in 30 years), but I don't know any of those people personally. What I *have* seen, however, are investors who relentlessly chase the dream of buying the **next** Apple, or the **next** Google. Sadly, most of them go broke in the trying.

What happens when people try to capture all three of money's golden qualities in one single investment — perfect liquidity, perfect growth potential and absolute safety? They meet with the same disappointment as the next Apple/Google dream chasers. Why? Because it doesn't exist. All three qualities have different goals and supporting strategies. The results of such a quest will be unpredictable at best and disastrous at worst. It is only by seeking the golden compromise that we achieve the utopian investment.

Not too long ago, a recently retired 60-year-old school teacher sat across from me at the offices of Petros Estate and Retirement Planning in Jacksonville, Florida. She had managed to save $250,000 for retirement and had been turned down by several advisors because they said she didn't have enough money to manage.

She was a single mother who had raised two children and put them through college without any support from her ex-husband.

She had a great pension which, combined with her Social Security, enabled us to craft a retirement plan whereby she had a LIQUID bucket with $40,000 in it. We put $110,000 into a lifetime income annuity which would give her some protection that included home health care benefits. We planned to turn on the income in 10 years when she turned 70, which gave her $14,000 annually for the rest of her life. That, combined with her pension and Social Security was more than enough for her to maintain her present standard of living. The income rider had a unique feature — a "health care doubler" which would kick in if and when she needed such care (based on the government's definition, inability to perform two of six activities of daily living, or ADLs, such as toileting, bathing, walking, feeding, dressing and continence). This provision would boost her income from $14,000 annually to $28,000 annually if she qualified. We weren't done. We put $100,000 in the GROWTH bucket to be conservatively managed to offset the effects of inflation and any other contingency that may come along.

The woman had been in total fear of retirement because she had been convinced she was bound to end up in poverty — a fear prompted by her dealings with other investment advisors who understood investing but not planning. When it began to sink in that her golden years would be free of worry, and that she had a guaranteed income that she couldn't outlive regardless of what the stock market did or didn't do, she couldn't stop tears from forming in her eyes.

Honestly, as unprofessional as it may have seemed, my eyes became a little moist as well, a phenomenon that often occurs when I see my clients begin to experience the reality of their retirement dreams. It made me remember why I chose this profession to begin with. It had nothing to do with numbers on a page or lines on a graph. It had more to do with the improvements I could help people make in their lives. It had more to do with my helping them achieve the dreams many of them had spent four decades working toward.

At the Woman's Worth® Total Well Being presentation, it's more than the money — it's about total well-being!

CHAPTER 5

Playing in the Red Zone of Retirement

I n football terms, the red zone is the last 20 yards before the goal line. What makes the red zone different from the rest of the field? The closer you are to the goal line, your approach to the game must change. Offensive coaches call it "playing on a shorter field." They have special plays drawn up just for this area of the field. The cardinal rule that every coach drums into his players is, whatever you do, don't fumble the ball in the red zone. Many a game has been won and lost by a mistake by either team when the goal is within sight.

In football, a touchdown is scored when the nose of the football crosses the plane of the goal line. Sometimes the ball carrier will stretch the ball out with one hand to break the plane. When this happens, all it takes to lose the ball is for a defensive player to swat it free. Most coaches recommend conservative play in this area of the field. Runners are told to tuck the ball securely under their arms. Quarterbacks are told to hold the ball with both hands until they throw it or hand it off.

So what is the "red zone" of retirement? It's when you are within 10 years or so of retiring. This is when the financial ball-game changes big time. This is no time to play fast and loose with your savings and risk losing all that you have worked for. The strategy called for here is "advance but protect." Keep your money growing, but not at the expense of safety. The ball is your retirement income, and taking your eye off the ball can cause you to lose it at the worst possible moment.

Red Zone Challenges

There are several critical challenges to your financial security once you enter this special area leading up to and into retirement. See if you don't agree.

Longevity — As we discussed in Chapter Three, people are living longer these days. That necessitates planning smarter to accommodate for those extra years of life. The alternative is running the risk of outliving your resources and losing your independence. No one relishes the idea of becoming a burden on their loved ones in old age. To prevent this from happening, you must have guaranteed income strategies. If you are 65 and married, there is a good chance that you or your spouse will live into your 90s. Are you prepared for that?

Rising Costs — When you retire, you will have severed yourself from a weekly paycheck. From now on, your pay will come from your investments and your savings. You may be ready for that according to today's expenses, but what about next year and the year after that? Do you expect taxes, health care and interest rates to go up? You are not alone. Most analysts agree that they will all rise in the future. Are your reserves healthy enough to compensate for those increases? Here's a scary thought for you: If the U.S. Congress were to close the deficit, federal taxes could double! How prepared are you for an eventuality such as that? You may have a retirement budget worked out with a good measure of flexibility, but what if you incur some expenses that weren't on the list, such as long-term care? Or what if Medicare cutbacks and routine medical costs increase 7 percent per year compounded during retirement? In the red zone, you need a plan that addresses at least a portion of these contingencies. One estimate says that an average healthy couple will need $260,000 to cover the eventuality of escalating health care costs over a 20-year retirement span — and that doesn't include long-term care costs. As of this writing, the 2015 Cost of Care report has long-term care costs of $91,000 as the national annual average.

Market Uncertainty — What impact will the volatility of the stock market have on your retirement? According to the Investment Company Institute, a trade group for mutual funds, 29 percent of those ages 55 to 59 have 100 percent of the money in their Individual Retirement Accounts invested in the stock market. Twenty-five percent of those between 60 and 64 have all their IRAs invested in stocks. What will happen to those folks when they are no longer contributing to their retirement accounts but making withdrawals from them? Every downward tick of the market serves to slice deeper into their non-renewable financial resources. In retirement, you need to avoid losses; the gain required to recover from a loss is exponential AND a relatively smaller loss can erase big gains. What's the first rule of investing? Never lose money! What's the second rule of investing? Follow the first rule. What does it take to recover? A 40 percent loss will require a 67 percent gain just to get back to even. A 60 percent loss will require a 150 percent gain to recover. You don't have time in retirement to recover from market losses so protect yourself wisely.

Red Zone Strategies

When you approach retirement, if you haven't already, it is time to develop strategies to protect your income in down markets and provide opportunities for growth when the market is up and guarantee yourself an income you cannot outlive.

Take Sally and Tom (not their real names) for example. Sally is 57 and Tom is 51. Sally unexpectedly lost her job after 17 years with a software company. Tom wants to work two more years and then retire. Together they have saved about $1 million, of which 90 percent is taxable. In order to maintain their current lifestyle throughout retirement, Sally and Tom will need around $1.8 million when they retire.

Because they started planning early, we created strategies for Sally and Tom that laddered annuities to protect their assets and provide income. We addressed rising health care costs and the potential for long-term care by selecting annuities with some home health care benefits built in. We protected them against the probability of increasing taxes for the surviving spouse by creating a life insurance program that would protect for lost pension and Social Security income should one spouse precede the other in death. The life insurance program also has built-in long-term care coverage included just in case.

In this case, proper planning included conservative asset allocation along with annuity and insurance solutions. That may not be the right mix for everyone, but for Sally and Tom it fit. Now they can fulfill their dream and never worry about running out of money. They can live their retirement with great confidence.

Red Zone Mistakes

Not Planning — Most people don't plan to fail at retirement; they just fail to plan. But it amounts to the same thing. It's what I call "ostrich syndrome." The ostrich, when it sees danger, sticks its head in the sand and pretends the danger doesn't exist. When we ignore the challenges of retirement we invite their consequences.

Waiting Until You Retire — Procrastination is a human phenomenon. Squirrels know instinctively that the time to gather nuts is prior to the snowfall. The simple truth is, the earlier you begin planning, the more effective your plan will be and the more successful your retirement will be. In contrast, the longer you wait the less effective your plan will be.

Improper Asset Allocation — Some people take inordinate risks with their portfolio because they have lost track of time. A better way to put it is they don't know where they are on the financial timeline of life. The investment methods and strategies that got you to retirement won't get you through retirement. It's time to change gears and become more conservative.

Not Anticipating Fumbles — Let's face it; life happens whether or not we are ready. Have an emergency fund equal to at least six to nine months of income. The fund needs to be liquid. A checking account, savings account, money market or CD will do nicely. If you should lose your job, break a leg, leave the gas burner on and burn the house down, there will be temporary financial consequences. Having an emergency fund keeps you from dipping into your savings.

I am sometimes asked: "If someone finds themselves in the financial 'red zone' and still doesn't have a true retirement plan in place, is it too late for them?" Well, earlier is better — much better, in fact — but it's never too late. There are customized recovery strategies we can employ. As long as there is a tomorrow, we can always plan for it. I am thoroughly convinced that people over the age of 50 need a retirement plan or they run the serious risk of running out of money before they run out of life. In fact, I can almost guarantee it, based on what I have seen. The $260,000 that recent data suggests that the average retiree will need to cover rising medical expenses over the next 20 years is anticipating changes to Medicare, to private and public health plans, higher co-pays, higher prescription drug costs, higher costs for diagnostic tests that will not be covered by Medicare and the layers of bureaucracy you will have to slice through to obtain the medical services you need.

Addressing Our Fears

When I was in the corporate world I worked with a woman who had a fear of flying. She was well educated and very intelligent. In most other areas of life she was courageous, but the idea of hurtling through the air, strapped in a seat bolted to the floor of an aluminum tube with wings gave her panic attacks. I knew this was a serious phobia with her when she insisted on driving more than 600 miles to an important business meeting when the company was picking up the tab for the airfare. So I approached her and asked her about her fears.

"I know it sounds silly," she said, "but the whole thing just frightens me to death."

I knew better than to try to reassure her with statistics, or repeat the tired old song that flying is five times safer than driving. I did make a recommendation, however. I suggested that she just spend a day hanging out at the airport just watching the planes take off and land. Watch the expressions of people as they exited the terminal. Did they appear as if they had just had the fright of their lives, or did it seem as if it were just an everyday thing? I recommended that while she was at the airport to ask some of people who had worked at the terminal for several years how many accidents they had witnessed. I didn't know if any of that would change her mind, but it was my way of trying to help. Her feelings may have been irrational, but they were her feelings, and feelings are facts.

As it turns out, she didn't take any of my suggestions. She still preferred to spend a long day behind the wheel rather than subject herself to the terror of flight. But she thanked me profusely for showing an interest in her and taking her fears seriously. She said most people ridiculed her without offering to help.

If you are approaching retirement you have a brand new set of concerns that previous generations never had to worry about, but you may have some unfounded fears, too. For example, some elect to begin taking their Social Security as soon as they turn 62 when they don't really need the income. When you ask them why they made that choice, they usually express the fear that, at the rate things are going and the size of the national debt, Social Security won't be around much longer. This is an irrational, unfounded fear. While it is true that Social Security must undergo some changes in order for it to still provide for the sons and daughters of baby boomers, the boomers themselves are OK.

I have come to the conclusion that most unfounded fears are borne from either misinformation or lack of information. A competent retirement planner will be able to educate you on some of these basic concerns and assuage them. When should you start taking Social Security? If you are healthy and expect to live at least to average life expectancy, in most cases it is best to wait until age 70. Why then? Because the benefit amount you stand to receive from Uncle Sam increases by 8 percent every year that you delay. When you reach age 70, there is no point in waiting any longer, however. Social Security is income for life. You want to get the most out of it and maybe it's best for you to take it at the full retirement age of 66, or perhaps if you are married, one of you takes it early and one defers. Every individual has a unique set of life circumstances that should dictate when to take this ever-so-important benefit. Let me repeat that each situation is different. A face-to-face conference with a caring and competent advisor who is interested in your fears and can educate you as to which ones are valid, and which ones are not, will clear the air very quickly.

Some have legitimate fears about long-term care. Statistics say that 70 percent of those over the age of 65 will need some form of long-term care. But they may have waited until they are well into their 60s before thinking seriously about it. By that time, the premiums on traditional long-term care policies are so high that it becomes a case of diminishing returns to carry it. One reason for their hand-wringing is that they are uninformed as to the many strategies that have come along in the last few years. Alternatives to traditional long-term care through annuity riders and certain life insurance contracts have significantly changed the long-term care coverage landscape. A little education in this area from a competent, caring financial advisor who specializes in retirement planning can ease those concerns considerably. If you are expressing some of these concerns and all your advisor can talk about are investments, you need to find a new advisor. You deserve answers about your future and you may be missing something you need to know to have a successful retirement.

Investing and Planning

The difference between planning and investing is simple. Investing is determining where your money will sit and grow until you need it. If done intelligently, investing will consider your time horizon. Regardless of what stage of life you find yourself in, all investing should be done using a goal-oriented model.

Planning, on the other hand, is a discipline. It allows you to look into the future with special eyewear, as it were, and see tomorrow from a financial perspective. You are able to pinpoint all the costs and income sources and lay the tracks for where you want your locomotive to go. Planning spies out the land of the future, anticipates challenges and equips you to effectively deal with them. It is much broader than simply addressing money matters. It involves addressing all things that impact you financially.

Running out of Money

In Chapter Two, we established that running out of money is the No. 1 fear among retiring baby boomers. A well-defined financial plan can cancel out that fear. When Genworth Financial did a survey on retirement readiness in 2012, they found Americans were retiring earlier but were underestimating how much it would cost them. According to the Genworth study, 52 percent of pre-retirees said they expected their expenses to decrease once they retired. Once in retirement, however, 65 percent of retirees reported an unexpected rise in expenses, mainly due to health care costs and caring for dependents. The Genworth pollsters found that only 12 percent of retirees said they would have enough money to meet those higher costs.

The November 11, 2013, edition of *The Street* featured an article by Brian O'Connel entitled "Americans Retiring Early, Then Running out of Money." Writing about the Genworth survey, O'Connel states:

> *"Put it all together and you have a scenario in which millions of Americans will retire not knowing they lack the necessary funds to survive in retirement — and may not have the financial means to close that money gap in their 60s, 70s and beyond."*

A Canadian Broadway entertainer enjoys a night with Petros clients at our Music of the Night Client Appreciation Gala.

CHAPTER 6

Other Critical Success Factors for Your Retirement

A s I write this, I am looking at a desktop (a real desktop, not a computer screen) with at least 10 pounds of periodicals and brochures about retirement in my unopened mail. Staying current with what's happening in the financial world demands a few hours a week scanning headlines and keeping up with the latest developments. Most of these magazines are trade journals with articles written either by or for retirement income planners. Some are brochures from companies.

It is easy to tell if the subject of a piece of reading material is about retirement just by looking at the illustrations that accompany it. They all seem to have a common thread. Here is a handsome 50-something man and a lovely 50-something woman, presumably his wife, strolling on a white, sandy beach with sea oats in the foreground and waves breaking gently in the background. They both have the requisite salt-and-pepper hair — not too young, not too old. They are dressed in smart, casual outfits — khakis, jeans and sweaters. If you look closely at these photographs, you notice that these people have perfect teeth and permanent smiles.

Sometimes they smile at each other, sometimes at a dog (nothing says happy retirement like a Cocker Spaniel or a Labrador Retriever), or sometimes they smile at their grandchildren playing in the distance. I call these people "happy preppie retirement models." They look as if they haven't a care in the world. In one, a couple is leaving a tennis court, holding hands. I *assume* they are leaving the tennis court because their tennis racquets are on their shoulders. Curiously, though, there is not one bead of sweat on them, so they may be just showing up to play. Whatever the case, they also have gleaming teeth and are smiling at each other. The obvious inference is that these are happy people, and don't you want to be like them? Well, of course you do!

Happiness in retirement depends upon a lot of things, and not all of them have a dollar sign attached to them. Since this is a financial book, I must make the observation that having an adequate supply of money may not make you happy in and of itself, but it is far better than the alternative! Still, some of the other "success factors" of retirement that have little to do with money deserve our consideration.

Social Connections — Do all or most of your social connections revolve around your job? If so, what will your social life be like when you retire? How will you continue to stay socially connected so that you don't end up as a hermit once you stop going to work every day? Unfortunately, some retirees cut ties with their workplace only to discover that their entire social life has disappeared, and they have few relationships to replace the ones they enjoyed with the crew they left behind. This can lead to depression, loneliness and boredom. Some have to re-learn the skills of finding new friends and cultivating new relationships.

The office was a natural common ground. So now what? Well, birds of a feather still flock together, and people with common interests are attracted to each other. Even widowhood brings loneliness in more ways than a loss of a spouse. Many of my widowed clients tell me that they no longer feel comfortable with the crowd they hung around with because their crowd is now all couples and they feel awkward. The key is to develop those common interests. You may find it in family members. Some have told me that during the time they were immersed in their careers, they didn't have as much time for cousins, aunts, uncles and even relatives in their immediate family, such as brothers and sisters, as they did once they retired. They found rekindling those relationships the natural thing to do. New friendships can come from former classmates. The internet, email and social networking have spawned millions of renewed relationships across the country. Deep and abiding friendships, once thought forever lost, have blossomed again through the magic of websites like Facebook and Instagram.

The thing about solid friendships is they don't happen overnight, and they have to happen naturally. It often starts with your being willing to meet new people and show a sincere interest in them and their lives. Listen to their stories and have fun with it.

I know of one couple who are the same age and retired the same month. They said, other than a few family members, they found they had few close friends once they retired. All that changed, however, when they joined a road cycling club and made many new friends when they signed up for long-distance touring rides. A couple of sailing enthusiasts found boating buddies when they signed up for a flotilla cruise in the Caribbean. Other ways to make new friends may include:

- Church groups — Remember those bus tours you never had time to go on when you were working? Now you have time, and it's an opportunity to meet new people.
- Volunteer — Develop your social skills while you are also doing something good for your community.
- Join a club — Book clubs, sports clubs, dancing clubs, country clubs… all are spawning grounds for new relationships.

- Pets — I'm serious! Many a friendship has been forged when walking the dog. The dogs get acquainted on greenways and parks, and their owners follow suit.
- Take a class — You always knew you could paint, and now there is a community college course near your home.
- Alumni Associations — You were much too busy to do this when you were in mid-career, but now that you have retired, find out if that college alumni association still meets on a regular basis. Rehashing the "good old days" is a perfect launching pad for new relationships.

Physical Activity — I attended a work conference once where the corporation had hired a motivational speaker. At everyone's place setting there was a plastic disc about the size of a half-dollar with the word "TUIT" printed on it in gold lettering. During her speech, she said that there were probably many things in life that we were going to do "when we got around to it."

"You no longer have an excuse to put off doing those things," she said, holding up the blue plastic disc, "because now you have a round 'TUIT'."

Maybe you are one of those people who found the time to keep yourself in great physical shape during your working years, but you are the exception rather than the rule. Regardless, once you retire you have time to pay more attention to the physical side of life. Exercise and eating right are the twin towers that support a healthy body as we age. The advantages to a healthy diet and aerobic exercise are endless. Among them are stress reduction, lowering the risk of stroke, heart attack and diabetes, not to mention producing a cheerful spirit and good attitude. After all, if you are going to live into your 90's, do you want to live "in sickness or in health?" Jackie Mason said it best:

"So many people spend their health gaining wealth, and then they have to spend their wealth to regain their health."

The vision of a sedentary Ma and Pa Kettle sitting on the front porch, glued to rocking chairs, watching the world slide by is so 1960s. Generally speaking, modern retirees are more aware of the importance of nutrition and exercise. Sixty is the new 40 and all that. Overall, health conditions have improved. People are living longer, and one reason is that they are more physically active — that and advances in science and health care. But nothing changes the fact that unless we use our muscles, we tend to age more quickly. The heart is a muscle. If we use it regularly, it has an easier time pumping blood through our arteries. Plainly put, physical activity helps us enjoy our retirement, and for a longer time.

Obesity is a challenge for older Americans. According to the Center for Disease Control, more than one-third of adults over age 65 were obese in 2007-2010. The culprit is our metabolism. It slows as we grow older, and we need less food for our biological machinery. If we don't make some adjustments in our diet... well, you know what happens. The experts advise us to weigh ourselves once a week, keep track of everything we eat and keep our weight reasonably close to what the charts say we should weigh. There are great websites that help you do this and integrate food with exercise. My favorite is myfitnesspal.com. It has truly become **my fitness pal!** It holds me accountable, which is something all of us need in order to enjoy our retirement years. I saw how important this was with a client who made a miraculous health turnaround. He was overweight and didn't have time to exercise or eat right due to his rather fast-paced work and travel schedule. We had put together a great retirement plan for him and his wife, and were right on track for retirement, but then he lost his job. It isn't fun when you are in your mid-50s and lose your job. Well, he was so committed to being productive during his job search that he hired a trainer, purchased a heart rate monitor and signed up on myfitnesspal.com. When I saw him three months later, he was half his size, looked 15 years younger and was an amazing ball of energy. He shared with me the power of taking life's disappointments and turning them into opportunities, and being productive when life throws you one of those curve balls. He is truly ready for a healthy retirement (but he has to wait because he landed a great job!).

The medical community reminds us that gravy is not a beverage, french fries are not vegetables and cake is not a food group! We are advised to choose fruits and veggies over candy and chips, and look for fish and lean meats on the menu instead of fried anything. Oh yes... and have someone who loves you hide the salt shaker and promise not to tell you where they put it.

Challenging Your Mind — The trials and tribulations of your career have kept you mentally sharp for years. How do you plan to keep your mental faculties sharp once you no longer have the mental challenges of your job on a daily basis? The old saying, "if you don't use it, you lose it," applies here. Our brains are like our muscles in that respect. You have to work out with it to keep mentally fit.

If you bought this book, and you have read this far, then you are to be commended for making deposits into your fund of knowledge. Reading is fundamental when it comes to staying mentally active as we age, and now you have more time for such things.

Scientists love to study the brain, but I think it is still largely a mystery to them. One article I read says that as we age our brain actually shrinks and gets lighter, and there is nothing we can do about it. Another article — and I like this one better — says that the "brain is pliable at any age."

Dr. Michael Chafetz, Ph.D., clinical psychologist in New Orleans, Louisiana, and author of *Smart for Life*, is quoted on the website www.MotherNature.com as saying that the brain slows down a little as we get older, but we can "stimulate blood flow to areas of the brain that are responsible for certain functions like mental calculations, language, learning and memory, just by exercising your mind."

Dr. Chafetz says that, in order to make the most of our mind's potential, we must "challenge it, stay socially active and believe in ourselves."

> "Even at age 60, 70, or 80, the brain is a work in progress," Dr. Chafetz says. "It needs constant stimulation to stay mentally sharp. That's why challenging activities are your brain's best friends. In fact, the more you can keep your brain doing things — reading, writing, traveling, learning new information — the more resistant your brain will be to the effects of aging."

Here are a few of the suggestions he offers to keep our minds challenged:

- **Turn off the TV.** If you are one of those who think most TV programming is mind-numbing, you are not alone. Researchers at Kansas State University in Manhattan, Kansas, found that people who watched just 15 minutes of TV had diminished brain-wave activity, an indication that their minds were turning off.
- **Flip open the nearest book.** Reading is a time-tested brain booster that helps improve language skills while keeping your memory strong.
- **Turn your head into a calculator.** Your brain will stay sharper if you trust it to add, subtract and multiply.
- **Anytime you pick up a pen** instead of the telephone, you help keep your mind sharp. Writing clarifies thoughts, improves logic and strengthens memory. Dr. Chafetz suggests you take a few minutes to write at least one letter a week to a friend or relative.
- **Take up an instrument.** Playing music brings an enormous number of skills into play, from improving coordination and concentration to fostering your creative instincts.

Just playing an instrument for 10 to 15 minutes a day can give your brain a good workout.

- **Allow yourself to shift gears**. If your favorite hobby seems a bit stale, your mind may be getting weary, too. So try something new. If you tire of woodworking, why not try sculpting with clay? Dr. Chafetz makes the observation that new hobbies require new skills; the development of which serves to energize the mind.
- **Sharing your accumulated lifelong learning** with others is a tremendous challenge and is great for the mind. Many community centers and civic organizations are eager for volunteers who can teach hobbies, languages or other skills.[4]

Look to the Future

Where do you see yourself five years after you retire? What will you be doing? During your working years, you may take a couple of weeks off work and travel to a destination just to relax. While that is enjoyable, it is not an accurate barometer for what a *permanent* vacation away from work will be like. From everything I read, it's not unusual for new retirees to experience anxiety and depression. Think about it. Here they have looked forward to this time of freedom all these years and when it finally arrives, instead of clicking their heels with joy, they have the blues and feel oddly restless and lost for no particular reason — at least not one they can recognize. One reason is that the image they may have built up in their minds — one sort of like the photographs on the covers of the brochures I described earlier — doesn't match their reality. I read the other day that retirement increases your risk of

---

[4] MotherNature.com. "Stay Mentally Sharp."
http://www.mothernature.com/archive/centers/detail.cfm?id=2958&term=Infection. Accessed June 2, 2015.

clinical depression by 40 percent, while raising your chances of being diagnosed with a physical ailment by 60 percent. I'm not sure about those statistics, but I can tell you from my unofficial poll that the happiest of my retired clients are not the ones with the most money, but the ones who stay the busiest after they retire. The ones who seem to have the most emotional and physical problems are also the ones who tend to isolate themselves socially. If someone thoroughly enjoyed what they were doing before they retired, and going to work every day was for them like going to a party, they will have a more difficult time adjusting to retirement. Nature abhors a vacuum.[5]

One gentleman I know worked 25 years for a manufacturing firm that specialized in making recreation equipment. He was highly successful in the company's marketing department and had developed relationships with parks and recreation department people in several states and municipalities all across the country. He had garnered a thorough knowledge of all things having to do with playground equipment, benches and picnic tables — just about everything you can imagine that could be found in a park. He loved his work and was good at it. When he announced his retirement, instead of counting down the days until he left the office and feeling buoyant about doing so, he dreaded the day.

"Leaving the job and the people at work was one of the most difficult things I ever did in my life," he would later say.

He played golf, and now he had plenty of time for the game, but did not find fulfillment in it. He got a phone call from one of his old customers one day asking his opinion about outdoor grills. He was happy to share his wisdom with his friend and former customer. The phone call gave him an idea. Why not become a con-

---

[5] Joseph Mercola. Mercola.com. May 30, 2013. "Retirement Could Be Bad for Health." http://articles.mercola.com/sites/articles/archive/2013/05/30/retirement.aspx. Accessed October 30, 2014.

sultant? He could stay involved and work from home and, what mattered most of all, feel as if he were able to contribute. It was a good decision. The business was successful. He was in charge of his time and was able to turn his expertise into a profitable commodity. This is what I call your "second act." The stage of life after your retirement can introduce to you a "second act" that you just might find more fulfilling and joyful than the primary career from which you are retiring.

An article entitled "Why retire? Become a consultant" by Art Koff appeared in the May 8, 2013, online edition of MarketWatch. Koff wrote:

> *"According to a survey conducted last fall by RetiredBrains, 'more than 8 percent of business professionals plan to continue working once they are eligible to retire'."*

The article went on to point out that consulting leads the list of businesses started by retirees.

Others I know have turned their hobbies into second careers. A woman who had worked for years as an administrative assistant to a corporate executive was good at what she did but not particularly in love with the job. When she retired, she found that she now had plenty of time for her passion, which was making pillows. All of her friends had decorative pillows she had made for them. They were the perfect gift for any personal occasion, such as weddings, birthdays and even holiday gifts. She would decorate her pillows with either devotional or motivational sayings to mark an occasion. She found a process by which she could turn photographic images into fabric images for special pillows. She never once thought of charging for her work until word about her work spread and strangers started making requests after she retired. Her little "pillow passion," as she calls it, turned into a small business that employs four people and produces a yearly catalog. She now earns double what her working salary provided and says she has never been happier.

Turning your passion into a business does not always require a particular skill. One woman was a devoted mother and grandmother. She loved children. When her own children and grandchildren had grown up, she found it only natural to volunteer as an aide at a local daycare. She didn't need the money; she just loved children and enjoyed telling them stories.

> *"God made some people with great scientific minds," she says. "He just gave me a big heart I guess. I love children. I love to tell them stories and make them laugh and take care of their boo-boos when they get hurt."*

When the day care told her they were going to close, she and her husband bought the business and the building that went with it. It is now a thriving enterprise with five employees and three vans.

Experts tell us that working after we retire can be good for our health, both psychologically and physically. The Transamerica Center for Retirement Studies has published a survey every year for some time now, and the 2014 survey found that the majority of American workers (54 percent) plan to work at something after they retire.

Since the possibility exists that you may want to go back to work in some capacity after you retire, I suggest that everybody have a fallback plan. If you do decide to have a post-retirement career of some sort, I hope it is not because you need the money, but because you enjoy contributing and want to find fulfillment. If you don't have a hobby or a passion in mind to pursue, keep your skills and talents up-to-date so that you have the option of getting a job if you choose to. After all, this is finally the time in your life when you can work because you want to, not because you have to.

What About Relocation?

You may decide to relocate. Some prefer a sunnier climate when they retire. Others want to move where it's cooler, or near the water. If you are one of them, there are several things to consider before making that move.

What is the tax situation there?

If you have been used to living in a state that charges no state tax, for example, it may come as a rude awakening when you have to pony up money you had not budgeted. Nine states do not levy an individual income tax: New Hampshire, Tennessee, Texas, Florida, Arizona, Alaska, Nevada, South Dakota and Washington. A word of caution, however. The states must pay for their public works somehow; so, many states that have no state income tax will have higher property taxes or higher sales taxes. If you have a pension, you may want to find out if you are moving to a state that taxes them. If you are contemplating a move, www.kiplinger.com offers a state-by-state guide to taxes on retirees. Also, it's not just about federal and state income tax but some states also have federal and state estate tax (a.k.a. death taxes — you even pay taxes when you die, and more of them, depending on the state).

Property values

Sometimes a move may make perfect sense on some levels and not on others. How much will the move cost you in terms of housing? The average home value in California is pushing $1 million while you can pick up the same residence in Arkansas for around $60,000. The cost of living in New York City is... how would Tony Soprano say it? "Fuhgeddaboudit!" Harlingen, Texas, is No. 1 on Kiplinger's 2014 list of the cheapest U.S. cities in which to live.

According to the report, the cost of living is 18.4 percent below the U.S. average, and the median home value is $77,700. The point is, if you are itching to change your address, do a little research. Several websites are devoted to rating cities and communities across the nation according how much it costs to live there. Talk to your financial advisor if this is in the cards and get his or her advice on how such a move might impact your retirement income plan. Make sure you run the projections, not only based on today's tax structures, but build in the unknowns. That's the only way you will be able to make a fact-based decision. Far too many pre-retirees and retirees make these decisions based on emotions not facts. This just isn't the time in your life to make financial choices without a plan.

Health care

It may not be an eventuality we want to think about, but what does long-term care cost in the area where you intend to live out your golden years? Costs vary from place to place. Genworth Financial does an excellent job each year of providing the costs associated with all facets of specialized nursing care in its annual state-by-state Cost of Care survey. The report shows the annual costs associated with assisted living facilities, nursing homes and home health care in each state. In New York, for example, the median annual cost for a semi-private room in a nursing home is $120,998 per year, whereas in Louisiana the average cost is $54,750. The bottom line: do your due diligence before you decide, and seek professional guidance if needed. Find out about transitional housing. Check out the cost of such facilities as continuing care retirement centers and active adult communities. If you intend to move into one of the retirement communities that are springing up around the country, speak with the activities director of these facilities and visit them personally before making a commitment.

I know how different the culture is in all these communities. This became explicitly evident to me one day when an 83-year-old widow asked me to help her find the right facility for her. I visited seven communities and narrowed the choices to three and then had her personally visit those top three. I had done my evaluation based on an understanding of her social needs, financial needs and long-term care needs. These were our top priorities. The selection was based on which one offered her the best quality of life and had a lively atmosphere. We talked and interviewed short-term residents and long-term residents; walked the halls of the assisted living centers, the skilled nursing centers and the rehab facilities; and also looked at learning and educational opportunities provided there. We ate in all the dining rooms, checked out the fitness rooms and looked into the other amenities provided. We also looked at the spiritual culture of the community. This was important to her since this was going to be her home for the rest of her life. This is the type of analysis you need to do before choosing a community. Don't just pick something out of the hat or rely on family and friends. Go and experience the community before deciding to live there.

Visualize Your Retirement

Try this: Close your eyes and visualize your retirement journey, not just the first year, but throughout its various stages. Don't assume anything, just picture yourself living life over the next two, three, or four decades. It's hard to do that without supplying details, isn't it? Where will you live? Where will you travel? What will you be doing with your time? We like to use a scenario planning model that involves just that type of visualization. You would be amazed at how many scenarios we can create that require making some simple decisions now that will affect our lives down the road and have major impacts and/or consequences.

Several "what ifs" appear when we try to imagine our retirement in detail. What if you maintained your current housing situation for 15 years and then relocated to be closer to your family during your later years? In the planning process, we put a value to this. It may not happen, but if there is a possibility of it happening, we want to be prepared. Why not put a cost to every probability? This will ensure we are making the most prudent financial choices possible. It is only when we solve the big puzzle that a successful retirement becomes a reality for you.

Other "what ifs" that need to be considered:

- What if one of us needs long-term care?
- What if we lose a source of income?
- What if our kids need help?
- What if we need to support one of our aging parents?
- What if...?

Create various lifestyle scenarios to ensure you are planning for the "what if's." Anything less is a recipe for unfulfilled dreams or worse, a retirement full of tumultuous events.

Petros clients enjoy dinner and learn from the Dream Team, our distinguished
Panel of Experts.

The Woman's Worth® Panel of Experts — sometimes I give them a food break!

CHAPTER 7

The Truth About Estate Planning and Legacy

The idea of what happens to an individual's wealth and worldly possessions at death has been a primary focus of the rule of law ever since the dawn of man. The Egyptians had a few sketchy laws on the subject. Whoever buried the deceased (presumably the next of kin) received what was left behind. From what archaeologists have unearthed in poking around the pyramids, the Egyptians thought they could take it with them. They found all sorts of items made of gold, silver and precious gems that were packed inside tombs and sarcophagi that suggest Egyptians fully intended to tote all of their worldly possessions into the afterlife.

Ancient Romans had a complex set of laws they called the "Twelve Tablets" that spelled out in great detail what became of the riches of one who died. Roman law dictated that, for a person's wishes to be carried out with respect to inheritance, one would have to, while still living, of course, designate an "heres," a word from which we derive the English "heir." If you were named an "heres," under the Roman code of Universal Succession, it meant that you essentially "stepped into the clothes" of the deceased and carried on for them. It was a heavy responsibility, because if the deceased owed debts, those obligations were passed on to you as if they were your own.

___

Strange but True

Down through the centuries, people have had different ideas on how to transfer what they had accumulated to the next generation when they died. From the believe-it-or-not department come these strange items:

- When German poet and author Heinrich Heine died in 1856, he left his considerable estate to his wife, Mathilde, with whom he had a tenuous relationship, on the condition that she remarry. He told friends that the odd bequest was so "at least one man will regret my death."

- Three men — a Polish composer by the name of Andre Tchaikowsky; John (Pop) Reed, a theatre worker; and Argentine businessman Juan Potomachi — made it clear in their last wills and testaments that their bodies were to be laid to rest without their heads. Why? Because they wanted their skulls to be used as stage props when Prince Hamlet, the character in the Shakespearean play by the same name, holds the skull of the court jester Yorick aloft and says, "Alas, poor Yorick! I knew him Horatio, a fellow of infinite jest." Well, I guess that's one way to get a role in a Shakespearean play. Apparently, the wishes of all three of the men were granted, probably because sums of money were also involved. On the other hand, Jonathan Hartman, a British actor who had always dreamed of performing in a Shakespeare play but was always rejected, left similar instructions in his will, but the theatre companies turned him down.

- Leona Helmsley, the hotel magnate, left $12 million to her dog, a little Maltese terrier named Trouble. She purposely left two of her grandchildren out of her will completely (for reasons she said they would "understand") and stipulated that the two who did receive small slices of her fortune would only receive them if they agreed to visit their father's grave frequently and sign a register to prove it.

- Beautiful socialite Sandra West, a California oil heiress, died at age 37 from an apparent prescription drug overdose. She had stipulated in her handwritten will that she be buried in a lace nightgown, "In my Ferrari, with the seat slated comfortably." Her will made it clear that her brother-in-law, Sol West III, could have the rest of her fortune but only if he carried out her strange request. She was interred as she had requested on May 19, 1977, under the glare of TV camera lights. The 20-foot-long grave was covered with a layer of concrete to deter car thieves.[6]

Even Stranger

While the above instances of inheritance gone wrong are bizarre, what is even stranger to me is why some Americans don't pay more attention to estate planning than they do. It is the one area of financial planning where the stroke of a pen (or the lack of one) can derail years of hard work and diligent savings and make scrambled eggs out of the inheritance process.

When some hear the words "estate planning" they immediately go looking for a couple of pencils to make a cross. It's not that

---

[6] Kit Carson. LegalZoom. December 2009. "The Top Ten Strangest Will Bequests." https://www.legalzoom.com/articles/the-top-ten-strangest-will-bequests. Accessed June 2, 2015.
Macy Halford. The New Yorker. June 3, 2009. "Skullduggery." http://www.newyorker.com/books/page-turner/skullduggery. Accessed June 2, 2015.
Ethan Trex. Mental Floss. August 27, 2009. "13 Bizarre Stipulations in Wills." http://mentalfloss.com/article/22633/13-bizarre-stipulations-wills. Accessed June 2, 2015.

frightening or complex. Whatever the size of your estate, you should have an estate plan. It could be as uncomplicated as having a few documents in place to tell your loved ones how to handle your final arrangements, such as a last will and testament. It could be a document that addresses such concerns as whether or not you wish to be kept alive artificially with wires and tubes should the situation arise or if you prefer otherwise. People offer lots of excuses as to why they haven't prepared an estate plan. To some, the word "estate" conjures up images of a mansion surrounded by acres of land. An estate simply means anything of value for which you have a purpose for after you pass away.

Because the idea of dying is depressing, some postpone planning for such an eventuality as if the very act of doing so would somehow hasten it. Others hesitate because it may cost them money. That's true; there are usually fees associated with a good estate plan, but the long-run costs to your heirs of not planning would eclipse any planning costs. Estate planning will require a bit of your time, also. But one of the reasons for estate planning is to keep your inheritance from being divided arbitrarily by the courts. The probate process can sometimes drag out for years if you fail to plan.

I have also talked to people who are understandably very private when it comes to their financial affairs. It is only natural to feel this way. There may be family complications involved, such as multiple marriages or strained relationships. If you are uncomfortable discussing sensitive family issues with a professional, it may be helpful to remember that along with the fiduciary relationship comes a pledge of confidence that is taken quite seriously. Confidentiality applies here just as it would with your physician. Just as you should not hold back discussing a physical ailment with your doctor, neither should you be reluctant to address sensitive areas of estate planning with a professional who is sworn to secrecy.

I have talked to some who feel strongly that passing on a large inheritance to their children will diminish their character. "I don't want to turn them into one of those trust-fund brats I see on television," one client told me. That usually tells me that I need to educate them a bit more regarding estate planning options available to them in this regard.

First Things First — Document Review

At Petros, once we establish a client relationship, the first thing we do, before we even begin addressing money matters, is to review documents — all documents — for the most common estate planning mistakes. You would be surprised how many people forget such a simple thing as updating beneficiary forms following a significant life event. When a client divorces or remarries, their designated beneficiary also changes. But if it is not changed on the paperwork of their financial documents, the account custodians, courts and insurance companies will go by what's on the paper. They can't read your mind. Take IRAs and 401(k)s for example. Owners seldom sit down and read through these documents. Typically, they are set to autopilot and seldom thought of until (a) it is time to withdraw money from them, or (b) the account holder dies. When a significant life event occurs, and the designated beneficiary line is not adjusted accordingly... well, you can imagine what could happen. There's an old saying in the world of retirement accounts: "The law of the plan is the law of the land." NO court of law will change that.

One case involved a couple where the wife died and inadvertently left a $1 million retirement account to her sister instead of her husband of more than 50 years. She was a teacher when she opened the account. When she married, she simply never thought to change the name on the beneficiary line. Decades later, her intended beneficiary may have been her husband, but her sister received the money.

What if an individual divorced and then remarried years later but never updated legal documents? That beneficiary line may look insignificant, but the information that appears there will be adhered to regardless of any other sentiment that may arise. In court proceedings, the designated beneficiary on a financial document trumps wills, trusts and all other estate documents when it comes to the dispersal of wealth at death. Let's say you divorced and remarried. Would you want your ex-spouse to receive the proceeds of your retirement savings accounts, your company pension and your life insurance? Can you imagine the incongruity of your fortune going to your ex-spouse's husband or wife upon his or her death? Or to that spouse's children whom you had never met? Remember, it's not enough just to update your will. The designated beneficiary form always takes precedence over your will.

Other Unnecessary Estate Blunders

Next we dive into legal documents that have to do with the proper and intended distribution of the client's wealth to heirs. We want to make sure they are compliant and truly represent the client's wishes. Once we step into this area, we find that many people have all kinds of documents that are not compliant. Each state has its own laws governing such instruments as wills, trusts and powers of attorney. These laws are not static. They change from time to time. If documents of this sort are not reviewed on a regular basis, it could be as bad as not having them in the first place.

Laws pertaining to estate planning vary from state to state. If you have your documents prepared in one state and then move to another, you will need to have an attorney in your destination state examine the documents to determine if they are still valid. In Alaska, for example, you can scratch out your last will in testament on the back of an envelope and, as long as you sign it, it will hold up in court. It's called a "holographic" will. Florida, on the other hand, will not accept such documents. For a will to be valid in Florida, it has to bear the signature of the testator at the bottom, and there must be two witnesses to the testator's signature. Not only that, but the two witnesses must be in the presence of each other when they sign. Any departure from that will make the will null and void.

What about oral (nuncupative) wills, audio wills or video wills? Maybe in other states, but not in Florida. Is a will valid if it is written in a foreign language? Yes, as long as it is accompanied by an English translation of same.

Florida Estate Laws

Another area where Florida law differs from other states is homestead laws. Florida places restrictions on whom you can and cannot leave your property to if it fits the description of a "homestead" or permanent private residence. Were you married at the time of your death? Were you survived by minor children? All of this matters. Let's say that you are not survived by minor children or a spouse — then you may leave your homestead to whomever you wish. Could you leave your homestead to a brother, sister or even a friend in this case? Apparently, yes, even if that meant disinheriting one or more of your natural children. If you *are* survived by a spouse or a minor child, the law becomes a little complicated and you will need an estate attorney to sort things out so your wishes will be carried out if state law allows.

Because of its abundant sunshine and more than 2,000 miles of shoreline, Florida attracts its share of move-ins, most of them from the northeastern section of the country. Through our part-

nerships with estate attorneys and other professionals, we have
been able to help many of them arrange their affairs to meet the
unique specifications of Florida law. In my experience, an estate
plan that was drafted in New York or New Jersey will not fly here
in Florida without a few adjustments. For example, there is something in Florida called a "self-proving affidavit." Many wills prepared in northern states don't include this. What is it? When a
will is probated in Florida, it is just another formality necessary to
make sure that the testator's signature was properly witnessed. It
requires that at least one of the individuals who witnessed the will
be tracked down. They must then sign a statement or affidavit
certifying that he or she actually witnessed the testator signing the
will. That makes the will "self-proving." If it sounds like a lot of
bother and jumping through hoops, I can't disagree. But Florida
lawmakers wanted to be sure they were sure, if you know what I
mean, and the law's the law.

Another area where Florida law shines when it comes to caution is the requirement that whoever is chosen to be the personal
representative of a Florida estate must either be a blood relative, a
spouse, or a Florida resident. In other words, you can have a bank
as your personal representative, but it must be a Florida bank or at
least a bank authorized to carry on business in Florida. What if all
your cash is in the First National Bank of New York? Doesn't
matter. If the bank is not authorized to do business in Florida, you
must select another personal representative.

Where this often comes into play is when the attorney who
drew up the documents practices in New Jersey and is designated
personal representative of the estate. They will likely be disquali-
fied from serving as a personal representative of the estate in Florida.

We are seeing a trend among our clients to look for professional trustees to distribute their estates for a variety of reasons. If
you decide to select a professional trustee, you want to do this

carefully. We see horror stories sometimes when financial institutions are appointed as trustees, and then the financial institution's trust departments become the gatekeepers. Beware of this because in the integrated planning we do, we work with clients to make sure whomever the trustee is will always act in the best interest of the beneficiaries. There are solutions other than naming a financial institution as the successor trustee. Often, it is in your best interest to select a "professional trustee" that is not a financial institution.

Another area where Florida is unique is its laws relating to powers of attorney. Who you select as your power of attorney in the event you are incapacitated will be able to act on your behalf. The POA is an important part of your estate planning. Florida changed its POA law on October 1, 2011, and added many specifications that weren't there before.

Essentially, there are two kinds of POAs: The "springing" POA, which means you must be declared incapable or incompetent before your POA can take action in your behalf, and the "durable" POA, a selection that goes into effect when you sign the nominating document. How could that affect you? If there is a time lag between when your "springing" POA can spring into action, paying your bills, tending to your investments and other affairs, the unnecessary delays could cost you in many ways, while the "attorney-in-fact," as representative in the durable POA is sometimes called, can act right away without awaiting orders from a judge or rulings from a doctor. We work only with board certified estate planning attorneys to make sure the structure of all of your legal documents are appropriate to achieve your goals while you are alive, and when you walk out on life.

Anyone who has a document pertaining to powers of attorney dated before October 1, 2011, needs to have it reviewed. Your existing POA was to be grandfathered in, but what we are seeing is that some financial firms are not accepting POAs dated pre-

October 1, 2011. Most financial advisors don't even look at your legal documents, much less ensure they are compliant within the state you reside and hold assets. At Petros, we offer this review at no cost to anyone who requests it because it is one of the essential components of your financial plan and cannot be construed as something outside of the plan. That's why we call our process "integrated retirement planning," and one of the critical components is the legal and estate plan — more on this later.

I could go on and on, but suffice it to say that estate planning is a state-by-state affair. I'll put it this way. If traffic laws were as non-standard as estate laws, we would have a difficult time taking a road trip across state lines. It would be as if the interstate highway on which we were zipping along just stopped at the state line and there was no connecting highway to be found.

Integrated Estate Plans

We are hearing the phrase "holistic medicine" more and more these days. There was a time, back when the world was less complicated, when the family doctor handled everything. You didn't go to an eye, ear, nose and throat specialist for an ailment affecting those parts of the body, you saw the general practitioner. Heck, in those days the amiable family doctor made house calls and even stayed for dinner. These are the days of specialists, however. You have one doctor for that arthritis in your left knee, and you see another doctor for the trouble you occasionally have with acid reflux. Unless they crosscheck thoroughly and often, they can prescribe medicines that can work at cross purposes, thus harming the patient's overall health. The word "holistic" means "whole" or "entire." Holistic medicine is when the medical treatment or advice takes the whole person into consideration, not one isolated body part.

It's the same (or at least is should be) with estate planning. An estate plan is not just a series of actions that are triggered at the end of one's life; it is a series of protective strategies that come into play at various points along the way while you are still living and **include** the exit stage of life. The effective integrated estate plan consists of a lifetime financial income plan, a health care plan, an asset management plan, a tax plan to manage tax obligations through the different stages of life and a legal plan, which has all the appropriate documents needed to protect your real property and your personal property. That's why we call the estate plan an "integrated" plan. It is, from a financial planning point of view, "holistic." It revolves around your unique view of your financial universe. It encompasses what is important and valuable to you and goes well beyond just the legal documents that have to do with your last wishes.

Estate plans are very personal in that regard. There can be no cookie-cutter solutions in estate planning. They just won't work well. And while do-it-yourself is a fine and acceptable way to handle a dripping faucet or emergency car repair, I don't recommend it for estate planning any more than I would recommend that you remove your own appendix. The way state laws are worded, the omission or addition of a word here or a paragraph there can change the entire estate landscape and send you down roads your heirs will not wish to travel. It's best to let the professionals do what the professionals do when it comes to these matters. Your legal plan should have the following primary documents:

- A will or a trust, whichever is appropriate
- A general POA for financial matters
- A health care POA and an attorney-in-fact designated to care for medical decisions should you become incapacitated
- A living will that spells out your end-of-life wishes

Those are just a few of the basics. As mentioned, the documents necessary for a good estate plan are as individual as a fingerprint. You may be a charitable-minded person, for example. In that case, you would need documents drawn up for that aspect of your legacy bequests. There can be any number of personal and family situations that will dictate the use of other documents along the way. I have been at this quite some time now, and in all that time, no two estate plans look exactly alike — which is as it should be.

Estate plans are fluid, too. They are not like books that, once written, are printed and shelved; they are living documents that must be reviewed at least on an annual basis, and most certainly when an important life event changes the family structure.

Estate Planning "Oops"

The word "probate" comes from the Latin "probatum" which means "prove." The only time we hear it these days, however, is in connection with a court process to determine who gets what after someone dies. The idea behind probate is that it is not good enough to leave a will with instructions on how you wish your worldly possessions to be distributed to your heirs. The public has a right to test the will and make sure that it is valid and true. The purpose, then, of the probate process is to officially and once for all time "prove" the will "in deed and in truth" to your last wishes.

From a financial planning point of view, there are some drawbacks to the probate process. Before we discuss them, however, let's ask and answer this question: Is it possible to bypass the probate process? The answer is: In many instances, yes, with the proper legal documents.

Now, here are the drawbacks to the probate process:

Probate can be time-consuming. The period between when the will is filed in court and the funds and property are distributed can be unreasonably long. In Florida, if everything is in order, the average time for formal administrations when there are no taxes due can be as brief as four to six months. But that is a big "if." The death certificates must be submitted. Only the original death certificate and certified copies will do. In Florida, the death certificate must be registered with the Vital Statistics office of the county in which the death occurred, and there are several signatures and authorizations involved with this process. Other issues that may consume time include obtaining the oaths of witnesses to the will, signatures from multiple beneficiaries, thorough legal descriptions of property and many others.

Working with the board-certified estate planning attorney that supports our clients, I sponsor free educational workshops from time to time on estate planning. I always like to ask the audience if anyone has experienced what I call a "probate horror story." One woman shared with the group that she stood to inherit money from her brother, she was the only heir to his estate and she was the executor. There were no complications that she or her lawyer knew of, and no claims against the estate. She said that it had been two years since her brother's death and she still had not received the money. I told her that she might want to look into hiring a new lawyer. The reason I believe her, however, is because I have seen it happen. Assets of the estate are frozen during the probate process. One reason has to do with inventory. If the estate is complicated and property, investments and valuables are involved, accountants and appraisers must take an accurate inventory. That can take time. What if the primary income earner of the family leaves behind a family that needs the money in order to pay bills and maintain its livelihood? It is in the judge's hands, of course, but his hands are often tied. He must obey the laws, which usually favor the probate process over the family's needs.

Probate can be costly. Probate has become more complicated in recent years, requiring attorneys to sort out things. Legal fees, executor fees and other costs must come out of the estate. Here's another strange issue — if the estate is spread over several states, the heirs may have to wrestle with the probate process in each of the states, thus increasing the costs. Each state has its own cost structure, too. There is no national price list. You are at the mercy of the courts and state laws in this regard.

Probate is public. What goes on in the courts is a matter of public record. Everyone who cares to know will know what was in the will under probate. Since the public will be able to see how much is in the estate, any remote relative, perhaps disgruntled because he or she was left out of the will, may freely contest the will and insist on his or her "rightful" share. The process actually invites such public scrutiny, since many states require the proceedings to be advertised. It's like the part in the wedding ceremony where the preacher says, "If anyone knows why this man and this woman should not be united in marriage, speak now or forever hold your peace." The family has no control. The judge (or the court) determines how much of the process is made public. Because of this publicity, the process can sometimes invite unscrupulous solicitors hoping to gain something from the estate, such as bogus debts they may claim the deceased left unpaid. I have heard the horror stories of hucksters who scan local newspapers so they can prey upon people who inherit money using clever investment schemes. Especially vulnerable to these con artists are young people who are prone to make unwise decisions when they suddenly inherit lump sums.

The fact that probate is public is something I take advantage of for education purposes. I let clients watch as I Google any famous person they name and get a copy of their will. I even have a copy of Anna Nicole Smith's will. It was faxed to my office one day by a solicitor using random fax numbers. Most people just aren't aware of how much of their family's personal information is exposed to the public during the probate process.

Contestability can be legal war. Wills are contestable and when feuds develop, the wrangling by family members takes place in the probate ring. In large families, it is not unusual for one family member to feel slighted and wage a legal war with his or her siblings that can drag out for years. What if the favorite niece is not mentioned in the will? She may join the fray. "Dad liked me best. He told me years ago he wanted me to have the bank CDs." That sort of thing. Some families have been torn apart, or the fabric of their bonds left in tatters over an ill-planned estate. The inherent contestability of wills may also invite tradesmen and contractors to file complaints against the estate.

There are many "probate horror stories," but some of the most fascinating involve celebrities. Perhaps one of the most notorious is the case of Anna Nicole Smith, the one whose will mysteriously appeared one day on my fax machine. Smith was a *Playboy* magazine centerfold who married oil billionaire J. Howard Marshall when she was 26 and he was 89. Marshall died 14 months after the wedding, but while he was alive, he showered the ex-bunny with expensive gifts and money. To her chagrin, he neglected to put her in his will. After his death, she claimed that he had verbally promised her that she would receive a portion of his estate when he died. Marshall's son by another marriage accused Smith of being a "gold digger." He spent 10 years refuting Smith's claims in probate court. Anna Nicole died of a drug overdose in 2007, and her lawyers argued that a slice of the estate should go to Smith's daughter who had been born just before her mother's death. But a federal court said no, that the billionaire had intended to leave his entire estate to his son. Adding to the irony, Smith reportedly stuck a paragraph in her will that expressly disinherited any of her future children. Go figure.

The death of Anna Nicole Smith may be the most legally complicated and litigious celebrity death ever and it could have all been avoided with the right paperwork. What's heartbreaking is her beautiful little daughter (if you have seen pictures I'm sure you will agree), who never knew her mother, has been a probate ping pong ball for all of her life, at least up to the time of this writing.

The Solution Is Proper Planning

The sad truth is that some people spend more time planning their vacations than they do planning for the rest of their lives and what will happen to the loved ones they leave behind. If you don't have a plan, you are leaving your estate open for all of the above. In summary, here are some practical preventative measures I recommend:

- Get with your financial advisor and have an annual review of your documents (of course this assumes your financial advisor does integrated planning. Many do not).
- Make sure the beneficiaries are correct. If a life event occurs, ask the professionals who are looking after your financial interests to help you ensure that you change beneficiaries legally and correctly. If you make a request to a financial institution that a beneficiary be changed, be sure to obtain a confirmation in writing that the change was made. *Do not assume* that they will make the change just because you told them to.
- Make sure you have the proper legal documents that protect your estate and agree with your wishes regarding it. For example, if an heir is on government assistance due to a disability, an inheritance could disrupt those benefits. Estate planning professionals can address these areas.
- A family trust may be needed. A trust is a legal entity created to own assets. Creating one avoids probate in most cases. It allows you to control the assets while you are living but transfers them to your heirs outside the public scrutiny and drawbacks of the probate process.

Tax-Efficient Wealth Transferal

One of the duties of a fiduciary financial advisor is to look out for the client's interests when it comes to taxes. The fiduciary advisor is like the guide whose job it is to (a) know where the tax traps are and (b) steer you clear of them. Make sure you understand how investments and property are passed on to your heirs. Many people think they want to reduce their taxes, so they start giving away their assets while they are alive. Their intentions may be good, but they may be creating a taxable obligation to their heirs without realizing it. Many non-IRA assets are eligible for a stepped up basis (the value of the asset at the date of death). This could be a significant savings for heirs. To illustrate: Let's say you have a home you purchased for $200,000. When you pass away, the home is valued at $350,000. If your heirs choose to sell the home, they should only pay taxes on anything above the $350,000 value of the home at your death. If you change the home to their names prior to your death, they lose this tax benefit and you may be creating a potential gift tax issue. This is one of hundreds of tax law provisions that a competent financial planner will be able to point out when planning your estate. That is why at Petros, we assemble a team of specialists, much like the surgical team performing a procedure. We work with the estate attorney, the Certified Public Accountant, the asset manager and anyone else we need to make sure we have addressed all of your goals, dreams and desires so you sleep well at night.

An integrated estate plan will merge living assets with legacy assets and make the transition seamless and tax-efficient. For example, annuity payouts for your beneficiaries can result in immediate taxation if not structured properly. This is why I prefer to use annuities for guaranteed income streams during your lifetime, but structure them in such a way as not to create an unnecessary tax burden for your beneficiaries. It's about proper and appropriate planning of every component of your financial jigsaw puzzle. The pieces need to fit precisely!

The Money Went Where???

Wouldn't it be a sad occurrence if your children's or grandchildren's inheritance were claimed by greedy creditors after you died? That has happened to some very intelligent people because they either received poor advice or none at all when it came to their estates. Just as you can't un-ring a bell, you can't do anything about the misplacement of your wealth after you die; it is only when you are living that your affairs can be put right. I was talking to a new client one morning who was rightfully angry. She had divorced her husband after a 30-year marriage but failed to update her documents in a timely manner. Subsequently, she received an inheritance from her mother. You probably know where this is going. Her inheritance was co-mingled with her marital funds and had to be included in the divorce settlement. Had she received proper advice and assistance from a competent financial advisor she would have been protected.

At a Panel of Experts event, no one can stump our Dream Team during the "Ask the Experts" portion.

CHAPTER 8

"Hope Is Not a Strategy"

"Luck is not a factor.
Hope is not a strategy.
Fear is not an option."
~ James Cameron

You probably know Hollywood movie director James Cameron by his movies — *Titanic, Aliens, Avatar* and *Terminator.* What you might not know about him is that he is one of the greatest thinkers of our time and is a consultant to the National Aeronautics and Space Administration (NASA). In a 2004 motivational speech to the space agency he concluded with these words of wisdom — "Luck is not a factor... Hope is not strategy... Fear is not an option."

That has become one of my all-time favorite quotes because it says so much about how things get done in life. It's not through chance and blind luck. We make our own luck by making a plan and sticking to it. I am amazed at the number of people who, when asked about their financial plan for retirement, answer with vague notions that boil down to little more than a whimsical hope that all will turn out well. That's hope. Hope is not a plan. You can't wish yourself into a comfortable and secure retirement. You must have a strategy in place with specific components and detailed action points.

Senior Citizens' Greatest Fear

What is your biggest fear? Heights? I know people who have to leave the room when a scene comes on TV of someone standing on the ledge of a building. They get nauseous just at the thought of such a thing. Others have a morbid fear of snakes.

In Chapter Two of this book I discussed the fact that 61 percent of adults, according to one survey, said their No. 1 fear was neither heights, nor snakes, spiders nor even death; it was outliving their money. In other words, living too long and running out of money. In Chapter Three, we offered statistical proof that people are living longer. If you are relatively healthy, your retirement could easily last 30 years or more. So, the horror of losing one's independence and becoming a burden on family or a ward of the state is not an unreasonable phobia.

In Chapter Four, we made the point that if you are age 65 and married, there is a good chance that you or your spouse will live into your 90s. We asked: "Are you prepared for that?" This is where having a strategy comes in. I don't mean to be a nag here, but what is yours?

The Global Positioning System (GPS) is a wonderful thing. Using satellite triangulation, a GPS can tell you exactly (within a foot or two) where you are. That is key piece of information No. 1. Key piece of information No. 2 is *where you want to go.* Where do you want to "go" in your retirement? Do you know? Can you visualize what you will be doing in five years? Ten years? Twenty years? Will you have the resources to make that vision a reality? When you boil it all down, that is the essence of a financial plan — to ensure you will have enough money for the rest of your life.

A friend who is a sailor told me how miraculous the GPS was in getting her in and out of harbors without running aground. As the boat moves, a red dot moves over a detailed chart (that's a map to us landlubbers) showing where the deep water is and pointing out all the shoals.

"When I plot a course, I don't just draw a straight line from point of origin to destination," she said, "I use waypoints."

She explained that a "waypoint" is a mark on the chart of where she plans to be at various intervals along her sail. If we are driving, we would call them "turn-by-turn directions." THAT is the difference between a plan and a strategy. The waypoints give you specific spots along your route where you will have to adjust course in order to reach your destination. There are several natural waypoints in a successful retirement journey; here we will list a few.

FINANCIAL WAYPOINT #1

Risk adjustment

As you advance along your financial timeline, you have to act your age. For example, our bodies will tell us whether we are capable of rough-and-tumble sports as we grow older. For most of us, there comes a time when we realize that it just isn't smart to risk our lives on thrill-packed extreme sports and we opt for more age-appropriate pastimes. That's why golf ranks as the favorite sport among retirees (and maybe explains why Florida is so full of golf courses). Likewise, we ought to gauge more carefully the risk we are taking with our wealth.

In Chapter Four we mentioned the Rule of 100, but it is worth defining again. Take your age and put a percent sign after it. It is that percentage of money that you should keep completely safe from market risk. The rest can be working for you at moderate risk. It's not a hard and fast rule. It is a rule of thumb, adjustable by individual risk tolerance and individual circumstances. I have seen far too many retirees fail to "act their age" when it comes to their money, placing most of it at risk in the stock market as if they had another 50 years to recoup their losses after a crash.

Recovery time

Skateboards look like so much fun when we watch teenagers frolic on them. But when grandfathers attempt to show their grandsons they can still "surf the sidewalk," bad things usually happen. People in their 60s and 70s should not invest as if they were 30 or 40. It's too risky. They may not have time to make up losses that are bound to occur. It's not all about the amount of sand in the hourglass, either. In your retirement years, you are usually in *withdrawal* mode, not *contribution* mode. When people estimate the gains they will need to recoup losses after a market tumble, they usually guess wrong. Here's an example. Recently, at a speaking engagement, I put a question to the group: "If you lose 50 percent in the market, how much does the market have to go up in order for you to get back to where you started?" You could almost see the gears turning above the heads of some in the audience, wondering if this were a trick question. Wasn't the obvious answer 50 percent? Down 50 percent, up 50 percent, you are back to square one, right? Wrong.

Let's say you pay $100 for one share of stock in a company. The stock goes down 50 percent. Now that share is worth $50. If the stock went up 50 percent, how much would it be worth? $75! The stock would have to increase 100 percent for you to get back to where you started, or twice as much in terms of percentage.

You have lived through some stock market crashes. They always recover, don't they? Yes... ***over time!***

Recovery time from a bear market

The stock market is cyclical and undulates like ocean swells, up and down. But when the market has a precipitous and prolonged downward slide and loses 20 percent or more, and the trend continues for more than two months, analysts call that a "bear market." They usually gauge a bear market as it is reflected by a market index, such as the S&P 500. Bear markets vary in depth (how much value stocks lose) and length (how long the losing trend continues). Investors who have time on their side can weather bear markets better than older investors. Here are some interesting statistics from Standard and Poor's about bear markets:

- There have been 16 bear markets since 1929.
- A bear market comes along every 4.8 years.
- The average depth of decline in a bear market is 38.24 percent
- On average, bear markets last 17 months.
- The average time it takes to break even (make up the losses) from a bear market is five years.[7]

Some bear markets and the recessions they spawn have been short-lived but deep. Take the bear market of 1987 for instance. According to some analysts, the approximate duration was a mere four months, but the decline was steep, as the S&P 500 lost 34 percent. It took investors approximately two years to recover from a four-month bear market, for example. Some may remember when the tech bubble burst in 2000. The ensuing bear market lasted from March 2000 to October 2002 and caused a drop of 49 percent in the S&P.

---

[7] standardandpoors.com

TIME TO RECOVERY OF A MARKET DECLINE

Period	Peak to trough decline of the S&P 500	Recovery Date	Time to Recovery
February 1966 to October 1966	-22%	May 1967	1 year 3 months
November 1968 to May 1970	-36%	March 1972	3 years 6 months
January 1973 to October 1974	-48%	July 1980	7 years 7 months
November 1980 to August 1982	-27%	November 1982	2 years
August 1987 to December 1987	-34%	July 1989	1 year 11 months
July 1990 to October 1990	-20%	February 1991	7 months
March 2000 to October 2002	-49%	June 2007	7 years 3 months
October 2007 to March 2009	-57%	March 2013	5 years 5 months
Average	**-34%**	**Period**	**3 years 2 months**

Source: Schwab Center for Financial Research with data provided by Bloombert. The periods shown where the S&P 500 fell 20% or more over a period of at least three months. **Past performance does not guarantee future results.**

It took investors seven years and three months to recover from that punch to the stomach. No sooner had they caught their breath than the financial crisis of 2008 hit, causing a 57 percent drop in the S&P. Recovery time was five years and five months. What's the point? Timing is critical to a retiree. I saw with my own eyes the pain and panic on the faces of those who had trusted their stockbrokers to handle their investments through their retirement years only to lose as much as half their life savings and it was difficult to watch them suffer. Many of them had to postpone their retirement for years and lower their lifestyles dramatically. Their problem was *timing!* Had they retired a year earlier, and reduced their market risk according to their age, they would have been fine. But the one-two punch of a sudden drop in the market and the fact that they were now in withdrawal mode instead of accumulation mode was a killer. The time it took for the market to recover was one thing. The time it took for them to recovery personally was another thing entirely. And, the toll it took on them physically due to the stress has yet to be determined.

RETIREMENT DONE RIGHT • 113

Realistically measuring recovery

When it comes to recovery time from a market crash, the charts measure peak to peak. In other words, if the market index was at 17,000 when it crashed, a full recovery will be declared when it reaches 17,000 again. But that is hardly the entire story. Let's say the time from crash to recovery lasted five years. When the market comes back to the point at which it began to slide is your account worth the same? Not by a long shot.

To illustrate the point, put four quarters on a table top. That is your portfolio. I am going to take 50 percent away by removing two quarters. You now have two quarters on the table. Now I am going to give you 50 percent back. How many quarters are on the table? Three, not the four you started with. To get back to having four quarters again I have to produce a recovery of 100 percent! That makes perfect sense with quarters, yet some people have trouble grasping it with their investments in the stock market.

KEY POINTS

Avoid losses: the gain required to recover from a loss is exponential; likewise, a relatively smaller loss can erase big gains.

Memorable Declines: what gain does it take to recover from these losses:

Dow	1929-1932	-89%	NASDAQ	2000-2002	-78%
S&P 500	1973-1974	-48%	S&P 500	2007-2009	-57%
S&P 500	2000-2002	-49%	Next ...		-??%

Note: "Dow" is the Dow Jones Industrial Average; Declines are peak to trough during the years presented

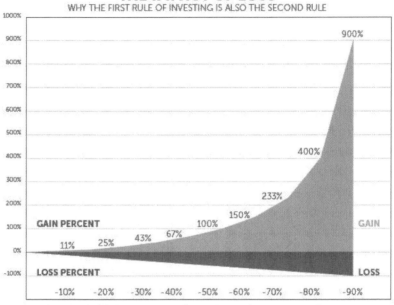

THE IMPACT OF LOSS
WHY THE FIRST RULE OF INVESTING IS ALSO THE SECOND RULE

Copyright 2009-2010, Crestmont Research (www.CrestmontResearch.com)

Emotions get in the way

Here's yet another factor to consider: When we look at charts that show the recovery time of the market, few investors will exactly mirror the movement of the markets because human nature and raw emotions get in the way. The age-old mantra of investing is buy low and sell high, but often the average investor does just the opposite of that. They will hang in there out of sheer stubbornness, thinking stocks will bounce back any day now, and the storm will blow over. When the correction goes deeper and longer, panic sets in and they sell at precisely the wrong time — just as the market starts to inch its way back. Even after it is clear that a recovery is underway, human emotions often prevent investors from capitalizing on it. The once-bitten-twice-shy syndrome kicks in and they miss the recovery because of their under-standable fear and mistrust of the market.

When measuring risk tolerance, give some serious thought to it. Sure, there are some folks who, like the professional gamblers in Las Vegas, are able to shrug off losses with an easy-come-easy-go attitude. And if you are one of those, then these words aren't meant for you. I am talking to those who have worked long and hard to accumulate what they have and wish to preserve it so they can retire in peace with a measure of financial security.

When we do our educational events, called our Panel of Experts, they consist of an estate planning attorney, a CPA, a health care planning professional, an income planning specialist and an investment advisor (this is what we call our Dream Team). Ryan Payne, who is the president of our asset management strategic partner, Payne Capital Management, and who serves as the investment advisor, always shares the six critical elements that provide the basics to building a successful portfolio in today's environment. This is a good place to present them to establish the foundation for success in retirement when it comes to your money management:

1. **Simplicity over complexity:** What this means is that convoluted money strategies that have higher costs and are tax inefficient in most cases lead to lower returns. Money saved in taxes is just as green as money you grow in the market, so make sure your money management is tax efficient.

2. **Compounding small returns:** Cash IS NOT king; compounding is! Compounding simply means your investment money is paying out dividends and interest, and those dividends and interest payments should be reinvested to buy more shares of your investments, which in effect pay out more dividends and interest and so on. The magic to grow-

ing your wealth is not only market returns but compound interest.

3. **Diversification:** Diversification is not having your money spread across two or three financial institutions, nor is it having money with two or three advisors. And, it certainly is not having all of your assets in only large cap stocks as we typically find. It's getting exposure to multiple asset categories because this hedges your risk and provides better return. Not all asset classes go up at the same time and they certainly all don't go down at the same time. Look at asset classes like a farmer looks at the crops he or she plants. If a farmer had to feed the family all year round, what would he plant? All corn? All wheat? No, he would plant multiple crops, including crops that produce a harvest all year round, and perhaps he would add in livestock. So it goes with your investments. Where are your crops?

4. **Expenses:** As Ryan says, "better the devil you see than the devil you don't see." Most of the fees in your portfolios are hidden — you most likely don't even know what they are or how they are impacting the performance of your portfolio. It is critical you know the cost of ownership of your investments and quite often the bigger fees are the hidden ones.

5. **Planning:** You don't need a one-size-fits-all investment portfolio. Your investments should be in direct line of sight to your retirement goals. It's the plan that should drive your portfolio to ensure you have the income you need to satisfy your retirement dreams and goals. This plan is not a "set it and forget it" plan. It's a living, breathing component of your retirement lifestyle. It must be looked at every year. Look at it as your financial physical; every year when you get your annual health physical, you need to get your financial physical.

6. **Invest for the long term:** Market volatility is here to stay. So, who do you think wins with market volatility? No, it's not the emotional investor! It's the long-term investor, much like Warren Buffet, who always buys and holds, whether we're talking about his companies or his investments. When the market pulls back, he's buying more — he doesn't exit. You build wealth by buying and compounding for the long term. If you can manage the emotions, you can manage your wealth and sleep well at night.

FINANCIAL WAYPOINT #2

Strategic diversification of resources

When you only have one or two eggs, it doesn't matter so much that you have them all on one basket. But when you accumulate a measure of wealth upon which you want to rely when you retire, it matters. You need to diversify, especially when you retire and the stakes are much higher and you can't afford to lose your accumulated wealth.

Some confuse diversification with owning four or five mutual funds, or having a portfolio with offsetting sectors. I suppose that is diversification to some degree. But the kind of diversification I'm talking about now is diversifying according to purpose. During retirement, diversification is much broader than simply owning a lot of different investments in your portfolio. I call them "money baskets."

Basket #1 — Liquid emergency funds. This is your "what-if" money that is the same as cash. You should have established such a fund early on in your working life, but of course it's never too late. How much? It varies. I touched on this in Chapter Five, but it bears repeating. One good rule of thumb is to take your monthly income before you retired and multiply it by six (months) at least — nine (months) if you want to be on the safe side. While it is OK to put this money to work for you, don't expect much in the way of a return if your money is 100 percent liquid (which an emergency fund must be). You keep this emergency fund available because the what-if's of life don't stop when you retire. What if the roof needs repair? What if the car needs replacing? What if you get sick or injured? Some may ask, "Can't I just use a credit card?" You can, but that would defeat the purpose. Then there is temptation not to pay the debt off immediately, and then you waste resources on interest payments. The purpose of the emergency fund is to allow you to keep your "untouchable" money untouched. We will get to why that is so important later on.

Basket #2 — Income you can't outlive. This is second in the sequential order of things because once you establish this basket, you are able to put other strategies to work to enhance your financial security in life. Remember the Rule of 100? Put a percent sign after your age and have that percentage of your assets safe from loss. It is this portion of your wealth that will be used to create a lifetime income. Once that is done, the rest can be used for growth.

How much income will you need in retirement and how do you make it (a) guaranteed and (b) an income for life? That's the job of your financial advisor (assuming you work with a financial advisor who has expertise in all the components of an integrated plan). Advisors who are retirement income specialists will hone in on what expenses you can reasonably anticipate once you enter retirement, and then they will go about the process of developing strategies that will enable you to have the income that matches it. Frankly, if you are not hearing those two key elements of your future income nailed down at the beginning of the planning process, (a) guaranteed and (b) lifetime, then you are speaking to the wrong kind of financial advisor. There are "accumulation" advisors who specialize with younger investors for whom retirement is years away, and there are "preservation and distribution" advisors who specialize in older investors who are at the threshold of retirement. The latter, of course, are the ones who are equipped to get you where you want to go with Basket #2.

Basket #3 — Growth. Once you have your emergency fund set aside and your guaranteed lifetime income in place, you can and should use the remainder of your assets for managed growth — at least enough to offset inflation, which historically averages around 3 percent per year. Inflation is like a pickpocket and a stealth burglar. You won't feel the effects of the slow erosion of your purchasing power, but it is there. The expression "safe risk" may sound oxymoronic, but it applies in this instance. The object of this portion of your portfolio is growth. To obtain this growth, you may have to expose this smaller part of your portfolio to a measure of risk. But because your guaranteed lifetime income is in place, the measured risk is acceptable in return for the prospects of growth. Your financial advisor will know exactly what this means and can help you put strategies in place to achieve it. But be sure you don't have ad hoc growth strategies. The growth basket has goals that are linked to your plans, not an advisor's plan or "stock picks."

Basket #4 or #5 — The unknown. You say wait, you just said three baskets. Oh yes, the three baskets are for the known. But then, based on your goals, you might need a fourth or fifth basket to provide for long-term care protection, to leave a legacy to your loved ones or to meet another unique need in your life. These can't be known without completing the integrated plan. With health care costs skyrocketing, with Medicare reform, with longevity, and the list goes on, we have to protect for the unknown. Remember, no two plans are alike so you may need this or you may not.

FINANCIAL WAYPOINT #3

Legacy and estate planning

This is definitely one area where you can't leave things to chance. Estate planning isn't as complicated as most people think. Nor is it expensive! The benefits of planning are incalculable:

- Eliminate tax penalties for your family.
- Prevent unnecessary fees and costs.
- Help your family distribute your estate's assets the way you intended.
- Take emotions out of the picture when multiple family members are involved.
- Allow your family to deal with practical matters during the grieving process.

Bottom line, you are able to control matters pertaining to your legacy instead of letting them come under the control of uninterested parties, such as the courts. Remember: ***If you fail to plan; you plan to fail.***

CHAPTER 9

Guaranteed Lifetime Income? Really?

I n Chapter Four of this book, I talked about the "4 percent rule" and how the behavior of the stock market in the last decade has debunked the myth that you can invest solely in the stock market all during your working life and emerge with a workable income plan that is guaranteed to carry you through retirement. That begs the question, then: Is there any viable way to produce a guaranteed income that one cannot outlive in retirement? Yes, there is. It is called by many names in the financial planning community, but the name that seems to be the most popular is "hybrid annuity."

Why Hybrid?

As everyone knows, a hybrid is a combination. A hybrid car is part gasoline-powered and part battery-powered. A hybrid plant is produced by cross-pollinating two existing plants. A hybrid annuity combines the safety and income-generating potential of a fixed annuity with the growth potential of stock market returns. In my opinion, these relatively new financial vehicles provide great opportunities for retirees, but I have to tell you that there are a few moving parts to them. You need to be sure you understand what they are and how they work before adding them as a piece of your overall retirement income strategy.

The misunderstood annuity

For some reason, in the 1960s Dr Pepper advertised itself as "the most misunderstood soft drink." I always wondered about that growing up. Why was it so misunderstood? And for that matter, how can a soft drink be misunderstood? You either like it or you don't. But, having been in the financial advisory profession now for a number of years, I know of no other financial product in the world as misunderstood as *the annuity*. For some reason, it's one of those things on which there seems to be no middle ground. Some people swear at them and some people swear by them. And everybody, regardless of the facts, seems to have an idea. Some very intelligent and educated people have some ideas about annuities that are frankly way out there in left field.

I once heard a caller radio listener give his opinion on a talk show where the topic under discussion swung around to annuities.

"Annuities are terrible... just horrible," the caller said.

"Why do you say that?" asked the talk show host.

"Because they are just a big rip-off... just something else for the insurance companies to get rich from at our expense," replied the man.

"And what in particular about annuities do you dislike, sir? Can you be more specific?" the host asked.

"I have heard that if you die young, then the insurance company keeps all your money and your family is left without a penny."

This was early on in my career, but I knew the caller had no idea what he was talking about. I wondered where in the world somebody who sounded otherwise educated and intelligent (the man was an aerospace engineer) could come up with such misinformation.

"What do you think of *this*?"

The hybrid annuity is the same as a fixed index annuity, which can have an income rider attached to it. According to insurance industry research organization LIMRA, in 2013 FIA sales were up 16 percent and totaled $39.3 billion in 2013. What is it that makes them so popular with retirees? The only financial instrument I know of that can provide (a) returns tied to the stock market and (b) a guaranteed lifetime income while (c) eliminating market risk is a fixed income annuity with an income rider.

Sometimes when I am before an audience discussing retirement income strategies, I will describe an investment without naming it. I will put the key attributes of the investment on a whiteboard as follows:

- Completely safe from market risk
- Returns tied to a market index
- Lawsuit, creditor protection
- Provides a guaranteed lifetime income
- Balance of account goes to heirs at death
- Eliminates the delays and unwanted publicity of probate
- Tax-deferred, compound growth
- Optional provisions for long-term care benefits

At this point I ask for a show of hands: "Raise your hand if you like what you see so far."

Nearly every hand goes up.

"Now... how many here like annuities?"

Only a few hands go up — mostly belonging to people who own them.

You see why I say, "Annuities are the most misunderstood financial instrument?" People like what they do, but for some reason they don't like the sound of the word!

Anyone who knows me knows that I like ferret out the truth like a heat-seeking missile and get to the facts. So let's do that with annuities and start with a little history.

Ancient Annuities

It is no accident that the word annual and annuity sound somewhat alike. When it was conceived, the annuity was a yearly payment. Annuities go back to the days of ancient Rome when soldiers pooled their money to ensure they would get a decent burial if they died in battle. An offshoot of that arrangement was a yearly stipend to families of slain warriors called an "annuitatem," taken from the Latin word meaning "year." Nothing scary about that, is there?

Annuities weren't heard from again until the 1600s when the French government sold "tontines," named after a Lorenzo Tonti, a Neapolitan banker who adapted the annuity idea as a scheme to raise money for wars. It was actually a pretty clever plan. You paid into a common fund to receive an annuity (annual payment) which became larger with the death of each fellow investor. The last survivor among participants received the entire balance of the tontine in a lump sum.

Fledgling insurance companies in 18th Century England came up with the first commercial annuity. Nothing complicated about it; you paid a premium to an insurance company in return for a promise that you could at some defined point transform the contract into an income stream. The idea was imported to America as a pension program for retired pastors and veterans of the Revolutionary War.

You may have heard of TIAA, the Teacher's Insurance Annuity Association. It was originally known as the Teacher's Pension Fund, an organization founded in 1905 by Andrew Carnegie, the steel magnate. His original mission was to provide annuities for teachers. The company is now known as TIAA-CREF.

Annuities became quite popular in the Great Depression. Uninsured banks were failing left and right and the stock market had crashed. Insurance companies, however, offered safe fixed annuities and investors flocked to them for security.

In the 1980s, the U.S. Congress passed tax laws allowing annuity owners to benefit from tax deferral. In 1995, the first fixed index annuity came on the market. More on this later, but it was an annuity that allowed investors to reap the benefits of an upward moving stock index without participating in the downside.

That's probably more than you wanted to know about annuities, but it's important to lay the groundwork for explaining how they work today and why they might just be the best thing since sliced bread and vanilla ice cream for someone seeking a secure financial position in retirement. Is there anything scary in what you've read so far? No? Then why is it that when some people hear the word "annuity" they run screaming from the room? I think I know why. Because most people don't really know annuities, they only know the **stereotype** of annuities — the way they used to be.

The best way I can illustrate this is with automobiles. Remember when anything made in Japan was thought to be shoddy and cheap? When you say Lexus today, what do you think of? Well-built luxury, right? Back in the day, annuities were like that. It wasn't that there was anything wrong with them; they just hadn't changed much since the time of Christ! You paid your money into them, either in payments or in a lump sum, your account received a small, predictable amount of interest, and at some point you could "annuitize" the contract — that is, convert the account into an income stream that would last for 10 years, 15 years or life (the longer the payout, the less the annual payment). At your death, the payments stopped.

The "old style" annuities got a bad rap because if you annuitized the contract and then died shortly thereafter, guess who kept all the money? The insurance company! The deal was great for you and bad for the insurance company if you lived to be 110. But it was a bad deal for you if you opted for the income stream and then died shortly thereafter. The insurance companies never apologized for this arrangement. That's just the way annuities had always worked.

Going back to the automobile analogy, remember when American car manufacturers were making great big gas guzzlers and the price of gasoline started to rise? And remember when the quality of American cars was so poor that the theme song for Detroit was "Shake, Rattle and Roll?" And remember how they finally woke up and admitted that if they were to stay competitive they would have to go back to the drawing board and retool? Well, that's what happened with insurance companies and annuities. In the final decade of the 20th Century, baby boomers were beginning to see retirement looming on the distant horizon but they weren't flocking to annuities. These staid, unimaginative contracts offered little in the way of return on investment for these younger, more market-savvy investors. They also were not fond of the use-it-or-lose-it income features of the old-style annuities.

It didn't help matters for the insurance industry that the stock market was booming in 1990s and there was no end in sight. Why go for something safe when you can put a blindfold on and pick virtually any stock and be almost guaranteed of a double-digit return — especially if it ended in "dot-com." It was the high-flying stock market that caused a few of the more progressive insurance companies to start thinking "outside the box." They called their actuaries and their product design people together and asked them to craft a new product that would combine the safety of annuities with the return potential of the stock market.

The insurance industry essentially said, "What if we took the things people liked about the traditional fixed annuity — the safety and income — and let returns be calculated from the growth of the stock market?"

"And what would happen if we eliminated the need to annuitize the contract to get a lifetime income? What if we made it so that the unused balance of the account could pass on to heirs when the contract owner died?"

Thus was born the fixed index annuity (FIA) with a guaranteed lifetime income rider (GLIR), or, as some insist on calling it, the *hybrid annuity.*

What's in a Name?

Now that we have the history lesson out of the way, let's take the name apart. Why are they called what they are called — **fixed index annuity?** Let's take one word at a time:

- **FIXED** — FIAs are "fixed" as opposed to *variable,* which is another class of annuities where your account is invested directly in the stock market. Fixed means you are safe from market risk and agencies that regulate insurance products classify FIAs as "fixed" for that reason. With fixed annuities you don't actually own stocks or mutual funds, which could go down in value. You own a contract with an insurance company that offers you certain guarantees. The next word in the name gives us a clue as to how an FIA can provide stock market-based returns.

- **INDEX** — Unlike the traditional fixed annuity, which has a declared interest rate that is adjusted each year, these annuities receive rates of return determined by the upward movement of a stock market index like the S&P 500, the NASDAQ or the Dow Jones Industrial Index. An FIA is not *invested in* those indices; it is **linked** to them — but only to their upward movement. Some contracts link returns to just one index and others use several. There are several ways to tweak the way interest is credited and you can make adjustments each year. One year, for instance, an annuity owner may choose to let the market drive 100 percent of the returns. Other years, the annuity owner may decide to opt for a fixed interest rate. The essence of it is this: when the index goes up, so does your account value. When the index goes down, your gains are locked in place. You don't participate in the downturn. Your account waits for the market to rise again and it will go up with it. That feature has received the nickname "ratchet-reset." Contract values reset each year and the worst you can do in a declining market is zero. Most FIAs work with *caps,* which means you receive the returns of the index up to a point. In other words, if the index shoots up 20 percent in one year and your cap is 8 percent, then you earn 8 percent. Caps are a tradeoff for not participating in losses. Some contracts offer *spreads.* If the index your contract is linked to goes up 10 percent, your account will be credited 10 percent *minus the spread.* If the spread is two points then your return would be 8 percent. In a year where the index is negative, your account will receive zero. Some contracts give you an option — cap or spread. I have found it makes little difference in the long run which you select, particularly if the goal of the annuity is to add the rider to provide lifetime income.

- **ANNUITY** — FIAs meet the standards set by regulatory agencies, such as the department of insurance in each state, to be called an annuity. Returns are tax-deferred, a trademark of annuity products. They have the capacity to provide an annual payout in exchange for a lump sum deposit, another trademark of annuity products. Like most other annuities, FIAs have surrender periods which are usually 10 years or so. If you withdraw all of your money prior to the expiration of your surrender period, you will pay a penalty for early withdrawal. A typical penalty will start at 10–12 percent and gradually decrease as the years left on the surrender period fall off. Annuities are retirement tools so I look at this penalty much like early withdrawal from an IRA if you are not 59 ½, because you end up paying a 10 percent penalty. Even during your surrender period, most FIAs will allow you to withdraw 10 percent of your funds without penalty. Typically, taxes are only paid on these contracts when the owner withdraws the money. Most of them are also RMD-friendly — that is to say, Required Minimum Distributions required by the IRS do not incur a penalty, regardless of the surrender period. Most FIAs also allow for a larger distribution if the owner is terminally ill or confined to a nursing home. Once the surrender period is over, no penalties are imposed.

The Income Rider

I find it interesting how much enthusiasm modern retirees seem to have for fixed index annuities. In 2013, sales of FIAs were up 16 percent over the previous year and totaled more than $38 billion. More than half of all FIAs purchased include a relatively new feature known as an income rider. This seems to scratch the baby boomers' itch for a dependable, guaranteed income stream in retirement. One reason for the popularity of this feature may be that boomers' parents had pensions to fall back on for income whereas most boomers do not.

Income riders are optional and they are not free. The charge is nominal, however… usually less than a percentage point per year. Think of them as sidecars on a motorcycle. You can have a stand-alone annuity (motorcycle) but a stand-alone income rider — well, like a sidecar, it just doesn't work that way.

Income riders are known by various names — guaranteed life-time withdrawal benefits (GLWB), guaranteed lifetime income benefit (GLIB) and the guaranteed lifetime income rider (GLIR). Perhaps you noticed the word "guaranteed" in all of them (it's hard to miss). These represent a huge break from brokerage invest-ment accounts, which, no matter how safe and diversified they may be, still work on *projections,* not guarantees.

Income streams generated by these riders do not require that you annuitize the contract and lose control of the account. Some annuity carriers provide for incomes to increase substantially if the annuitant is confined to a nursing home. While the income rider pays out, the remaining money in the annuity continues to grow according to the terms of the contract.

A look under the hood

I will be the first to admit that fixed index annuities with in-come riders have a few moving parts. But if you are considering them as part of your financial planning strategy for retirement, you need to understand them and know how they function. Let me put it this way: I am not a mechanic, but I drive a car. I am not a technology geek, but I use a computer. I call it having a "work-ing knowledge." If you are going to use these financial instru-ments, you need to have a working knowledge so you can feel confident and comfortable that they are a good fit for you.

Income riders vary from company to company but they all do essentially the same thing — guarantee a lifetime income stream. Remember, the income rider is a "side account" and works independently of the performance of the primary annuity.

Think of one account with two ledgers. One ledger is the **base account** — the actual annuity — from which you may withdraw money at any time minus any surrender charges that may still apply. The income rider is the other ledger which we will call the **income account.** The income account has only one purpose — to provide an income. You cannot access the income account as a lump sum. You have to take it in payments, like a salary or a pension.

When it comes time for you to begin receiving your income, how is it calculated? Naturally, the more you put into the base account, the larger the income you stand to receive. Time is another factor. The longer you can let the income account grow, the fatter your paycheck when you turn on the income stream.

The calculation of the payout is based on what is called the *"roll-up rate"* — so-called because this is the rate at which the account earns credit (just like the credits you earn in your Social Security payments by deferring to age 70) until you decide to activate the income. As I write this, the rate for most income riders is around 6–7 percent, compounded for the first 10 years. This rate fluctuates with the prevailing interest rate but once it is in place, it locks in. It is important to understand that the *income* account is not the *"walk-away"* money; it is used as a calculation base for income when desired. In most contracts, the amount of the payout is 5 percent of the value of the account perpetually if the payee is between 60 and 70 years of age. If the recipient is between 70 and 80, then the payout is usually 6 percent. This may vary slightly from company to company.

With most income riders, if the **base account** value is higher than the **income** account value, you may use the higher of the two as a calculation base. Once the income is triggered, that amount continues for as long as the owner or annuitant lives. It can be set up to extend for the life of the spouse as well, at a slightly discounted payout rate.

Long-term care benefits

Another relatively new feature with these types of annuities is long-term care benefits, but not in the traditional sense of long-term care insurance. These are optional and can be tacked onto the income rider provisions. This may be a solution for older individuals for whom traditional long-term care insurance would be too expensive. Some hybrid annuities now include home health care benefits as part of the contract. Some companies are coming up with contracts that will pay out long-term care coverage as part of the contract, with benefits based on a percentage of the annuity account value if the annuity owner meets the federal definition of long-term care. If the annuity owner needs long-term care, the claim is paid from the accumulated value of the base annuity. Whether to add these types of riders on the base annuity or not should be determined based on the integrated plan and your retirement goals and personal family situation.

Long-term care/annuity combos

Combination, or "combo," policies combine aspects of a traditional fixed annuity with aspects of long-term care coverage. One side is the fixed annuity portion of the contract, which provides a guaranteed interest rate. The rate fluctuates with the prevailing interest rate environment of the overall economy and is typically double if not more the interest rate paid on CDs. The other side of the "combo" is long-term care coverage designed to pay out two to three times the initial policy value over two or three years after the annuity account value is depleted.

For example, John deposits $100,000 into this type of annuity. He has a benefit limit of 300 percent and a two-year long-term care benefit factor. The first $100,000 of his long-term care expenses comes from his annuity. After that, the additional $200,000 is paid per the contract. Naturally, the more you deposit, the higher the benefits. These aren't for everyone because there is a measure of underwriting (your health determines your qualification). And there is usually a minimum deposit of $100,000. The provisions of the Pension Protection Act of 2006 give some tax advantages to this kind of program, also.

Necessarily Complex

I may have told you more than you wanted to know about annuities, but I would rather err on the side of too much information than not enough. It is impossible in the limited space I have in this book and your limited time as a reader to describe every little spring and gear of the fixed index annuity and its revolutionary income rider. It is a bit complex, but it has to be able to provide (a) safety, (b) better than average returns and (c) an income you can't outlive. A high-quality watch is complex to the average Jane or Joe, but the watchmakers understand them quite well. I have been in on the back-room discussions when actuaries and product design people meet to hammer out insurance solutions and I know how that process works. I have to remind myself sometimes that most people, when they ask you what time it is, don't expect you to take your watch apart. A simple "half past four" will do just fine. So the information here is broad-brush, with a thick coat of details. I believe the more you know about any strategy you use in planning your financial future, the more confident and comfortable you will be.

Not too long ago, I was at a dinner party with a few friends. The host loved to cook and presented us with a delightful meal which was consumed with enthusiasm. While most of us thanked him and complimented him on his expertise as a cook, one of the dinner guests asked him if he would mind sharing the recipe. He was glad to, of course. He even spent quite a bit of time explaining every little nuance of how the ingredients went together, the timing involved and the many subtle ways the taste was influenced by the process. It's a little like that with these modern annuities. I sometimes hear, "That sounds too good to be true!" That tells me the speaker doesn't fully understand FIAs. They are good, yes. But they are not too good to be true. Most people are content with the function they serve — sort of like the person who just wants to know what time it is. But for those who want to see how the watch works (or what the ingredients are), I am happy to share that information in great detail. "See me after class," as our teachers used to say when we had a deep question. My contact information will be on the back of the book and I will happily explain each little detail and make sure your curiosity is completely satisfied. After all, I am a proud owner of five annuity contracts as part of my retirement portfolio, and I can promise you this: I LOVE ANNUITIES because they are GUARANTEED.

Why the Annuity Bias?

As I am sure you have gathered by now, nothing disturbs me more than misinformation — especially when it is disseminated purposely. Some of the bias against annuities comes from individuals who are in the financial advisory profession but who would rather sell you on a product than solve a problem. Sometimes there is a profit motive involved, and others simply don't know these solutions exist or know how they work.

I encourage every investor to stay alert when it comes to accepting as gospel any point of view that seems too one-sided or extreme. Check the facts before you believe anything and don't believe everything you read.

An example of what I call "annuity bias" in some sectors of the financial advisory profession came after the financial crisis of 2008 when many saw how vulnerable their life's savings could be when exposed to a volatile stock market. Annuities were flying off the shelves the next year as American investors, especially seniors, sought the safety and guaranteed growth of these products. That didn't sit too well with financial advisors who were captive agents of large brokerage houses and could only offer traditional market-based investing strategies. Suddenly, articles trashing annuities began appearing in the pages of some financial magazines. Why? All you had to do to find out was look at the advertisements that appeared in the pages of the magazines. The ads were placed there by stockbrokers who wanted to stem the tide of investors moving sizable portions of their portfolios to the safety of annuities. It was becoming evident that those who had moved a portion of their portfolio to the safety of insurance-based retirement products were better off for the move.

Meanwhile, independent journalists began to say glowing things about annuities. A report issued by the prestigious Wharton School of Business in 2010, for example, contained a detailed study of fixed index annuities. The study was entitled: "Real World Index Annuity Returns." Wharton Professor David Babbel, who is unbiased in every respect, concluded:

> *"...guaranteed income annuities, which convert part of your retirement savings into income that will last a lifetime, are a viable solution to the challenges facing retirees."*

After the Wharton report came another report from a federal agency, the Government Accountability Office (GAO), that forthrightly said, *"...retirees need to purchase more annuities."*

Petros co-owner and Certified Financial Planner, Michael Macke, and I share some wit and wisdom in the recording studio.

CHAPTER 10

Conclusion

So now, do you get the full picture of "what all the hype is about retirement"? It's about protecting your retirement lifestyle and that is not as linear as a trend chart on an investment returns graph. The hype is that you spent 30 to 40 years dreaming about the retirement you wanted for yourself and your family, and let's face it, you have never been retired before, so planning for the journey that you will be on for another 30 to 40 years takes discipline, commitment and, most importantly, a team of like-minded, trusted professionals who are marching to the beat of your drum. That's why we call it Retirement Lifestyle Protection Planning®, and why I have made it my mission to transform how pre-retirees and retirees are served by the financial industry.

What makes us different? We integrate all components of your retirement lifestyle as discussed on the pages of this book. We pull together the best of the best of experts in estate planning, tax planning, financial planning and health care planning, and we become your retirement team. You need a high-performing team to get you through your retirement. It's RETIREMENT DONE RIGHT! Because you only have one chance to do it right... So, don't just INVEST... PLAN, because your dreams deserve the best!

ABOUT THE AUTHOR

Jeannette Bajalia is the president and principal advisor for Petros Estate and Retirement Planning based in Jacksonville, Florida. She was born in Jacksonville, and lives a few footsteps away from the Atlantic Ocean in Ponte Vedra Beach, Florida. After more than 38 years in the corporate world, Jeannette left her executive position with Blue Cross & Blue Shield of Florida in 2007 and launched her second career as a retirement planner. Since her mission has always been to help people improve the quality of their lives through her work, she views the transition from insurance executive to retirement planner as a continuation rather than a change of direction.

Jeannette provides counseling on a wide range of financial issues including lifetime income planning, tax reduction strategies, estate planning and investments. She is the author of *WiSe Up Women!* — *A Guide to Total Fiscal and Physical Wellbeing,* published by Advantage Media Group in 2012, which brought a woman's perspective to our Retirement Lifestyle Protection Planning®. Her cut-to-the-chase style of communicating and her keen insight into the financial landscape of retirement challenges and solutions have garnered much attention from the media. She has been featured in *The Wall Street Journal* and *Forbes,* and was selected by the *Jacksonville Business Journal* as one of 20 "Women of Influence" of 2012. In the last few years, she has been interviewed by major TV networks and has been seen on CNBC, Reuters, Yahoo Finance and MarketWatch.com. She is a weekly guest and trusted advisor on "The Financial Safari" radio show, which airs on WOKV, 104.5 FM, and has appeared on First Coast Living on WTLV. She has been published in such periodicals as *Entrepreneur Anchor* and *Health Source,* has been featured in both the *Florida Times Union* and the *Ponte Vedra Recorder,* and is a speaker for many area women's groups. She is also the host of a weekly radio program, "Woman's Worth® Radio," which airs in many geographic areas. "Woman's Worth® Radio" is dedicated to addressing the unique financial challenges women face due to longevity.

CAREER PATH

Jeannette began her corporate career at insurance giant Prudential on the day after she graduated from high school at age 16 and rose to a middle management position by age 21.

"My parents could not afford for me to go to college," says Jeannette, "so I worked at Prudential in a very demanding position and went to college at night."

Jeannette earned her bachelor's degree in three years while working full time. It took her two years to get her master's degree

RETIREMENT DONE RIGHT • 141

from the University of North Florida, again while working full time.

When she left the corporate world and approached Petros Financial Services to ask about a position as an advisor, she did so out of frustration. She had approached five other "financial advisors" seeking advice on what to do with her 401(k) account and the lump sum payout of her pension plan.

"Those I approached wanted to grab my assets and put them in the stock market without any planning based on my retirement goals or risk tolerance," remembers Jeannette. "And these were high-end advisors who didn't seem to want to understand me or my plans for the future. Under their system I would have no guarantees that my money would last as long as I might. I decided I could do a better job myself, if I only had the tools. I realized they didn't care about me... they only cared about my money."

Her quest led her to Petros.

"I had only intended to stick my toe into the water of financial planning, just enough to find my own solutions," Jeannette said. "But I soon became intrigued with the process. It seemed like a natural fit for me to take the training to become credentialed as a retirement advisor."

The timing was right and in a few months, Jeannette, now fully "un-retired" and back at work, was able to build an integrated retirement planning approach and in two short years buy the company. She changed the business model of Petros from a firm that only did insurance sales to a comprehensive, fully integrated retirement planning firm. Under her influence, Petros expanded to help retirees deal with retirement income strategies, estate and tax planning, health care solutions and insurance solutions serving Jacksonville, St. Augustine, Palm Coast, Orlando and all surrounding areas. Her success led her to launch another company, Woman's Worth®, dedicated to meeting the unique financial needs of single, divorced and widowed women, and married women who are the financial leaders of money matters in their households.

FAMILY LIFE

When Jeanette describes her family life, she speaks of herself as "first generation American." Her father and mother both immigrated to the United States and she was born here. Hers was a traditional family, deeply religious and rooted in Middle Eastern culture.

"I saw my mother take care of my grandmother for seven years after her stroke," Jeannette remembers. "There was never a question about it. That's what family means. My father passed away when I was 26 and I ended up taking care of my mother and my aunt until they died; my mother lived to 93 and my aunt to 101."

Jeannette describes her mother and father as hard-working individuals who were the epitome of hospitality, opening up their home to anyone in need. She says that they appreciated the opportunity America presented them. She has fond memories of working behind the cash register at her father's store when she was only seven years old and getting to know loyal customers.

"They loved the Lord and made sure we knew what was expected of us with regard to upholding the family legacy," says Jeannette. "They would not allow us to abdicate the values we were raised with. They were wonderful examples of 'tough love' and were relentless in teaching us values and morals."

ACKNOWLEDGEMENTS

My inspiration for writing this book came from the many men and women who so graciously opened up their lives to me during their retirement planning and continue to encourage me to shout out from the mountain tops that planning is the key to success and not investing. And so it is with great gratitude that I present this book to reach the multitudes to help bring clarity to the difference between planning and investing, and how the key to retirement success is the plan — not the investments. Thank you to all my clients who have allowed me to share their lives, their stories and, most importantly, their sorrows and joys as life events occur.

To my business partner, Brian Mickley, for so many years of putting up with my relentless pursuit of doing what is right by people, for people, and allowing me the freedom to discover, create planning models and help those who enter our doors while running the company, my deepest gratitude for your commitment and pursuit of protecting me from myself for my own sanity. And, to Michael Macke, co-owner and principal advisor, for your willingness to take the risk to step out of your prestigious position with your firm and join Petros to help us carry on with our vision and mission to help families preserve and protect their desired retirement lifestyle. These two men are the epitome of moral, ethical and God-fearing businessmen who uphold the highest standards so lacking in the financial industry.

To the Petros team, you guys are a class act. Words can't express the gratitude I feel for the work you do to carry out our vision and meet the needs of all those we serve.

This book would not have been possible without the tremendous support from the Petros Dream Team. I am truly blessed to be surrounded by an amazing team of dedicated professionals who serve our clients and have taught me so much about the value of our integrated planning approach. They help all of our clients achieve their retirement dreams, as we cannot do it without their unconditional commitment to protect individuals and families. This team includes Anne Buzby-Walt, shareholder and estate planning attorney at Fisher, Tousey, Leas and Ball; Nicholas Simonic, president, and Joanne Ratnecht, CPA and partner, at Simonic, Simonic, Ratnecht and Associates; Ryan Payne, president, and Robert Payne, chief investment officer, at Payne Capital Management; and the entire team of this amazing firm of highly talented investment advisors. I feel so blessed to have a team of strategic partners that are value-driven and committed to the same mission and vision we have at Petros. There are multitudes of other players on our Dream Team to include: the end-of-life planners, the health care planners, the mortgage advisors and many others who make it possible for our clients to journey through retirement with confidence and trust.

I also want to recognize my family and friends, whom I may have neglected while doing the research and the writing of this ever-so-important message presented in this book, and just know that you are the reason I do what I do; you have given me permission to be myself and pursue my passion and my ministry in helping individuals and families navigate the jungle of retirement planning. Thank you for enabling me to fulfill my commitment to the ministry of retirement planning, because I do what I do in fulfillment of my divine purpose.

This book would not have been made possible without the research and editing support of Tom Bowen, editor. His eloquence and encouragement to just be myself and write like I was talking, and his ability to make sense out of my words is beyond incredible. What a gift you are, Tom, to take technical information from a totally left-brained author and have it flow like music.

Most importantly, I want to thank my God, who has blessed me with the gift of being able to help people protect their retirement security and independence, and for the people He sends for me to help. It is through those that I serve that I can truly say, I am serving the Lord — hence, it is my ministry, not my career.

Made in the USA
Columbia, SC
31 January 2019